THE
FAMILY
CLINIC

PASTOR GODLY AGALA

PRODUCTIONS INC.

Published by
HeartBeat Productions Inc.
Box 633
Abbotsford, BC Canada V2T 6Z8
email: info@heartbeat1.com
604.852.3769
ISBN: 978-1-895112-63-4

Edited by: Dr. Win Wachsmann
Cover photo:
Https://Visualhunt.com/F2/13584554804/6C1EBAE9BD/
Cover design: Dr. Carrie Wachsmann

DEDICATION

This book is dedicated first to my Lord Jesus Christ who gave the Inspiration and the Grace to put it down for others to read.

To Phoenix University of Theology, now Primus University of Theology, Phoenix, Arizona, USA. You provided the platform on which this book was written.

To my adorable wife, Ndidi Paschaline, for being my personal home pastor. And to the children: Prince, Princess, Prosper, Precious, Praise, and Prisca. You have followed us closely in our walk with God. You all made my life worthwhile.

Dr. Godly Agala

TABLE OF CONTENTS

ACKNOWLEDGMENTS

My profound gratitude goes to this beloved family, Dr. & Mrs. Win Wachsmann, whom I met during my doctorate graduation in Phoenix, Arizona, USA. I will never forget how they said to me: "Pastor Godly we will publish your book and place it on Amazon." Wondering how they knew I had plans to write books, I became convinced that God wanted me to do something about the plan. They told me "just start." And by the grace of God, I started. Today, *The Family Clinic* is the outcome. Dr. Win, the electronic material you sent me on hermeneutics was very useful.

I am greatly indebted to the president of our prestigious Phoenix University of Theology, Dr. Karen Drake, in Arizona, USA. Your insistence made this a reality today. You even offered me the opportunity of co-editing the book with Dr. Win, in spite of your very tight schedules. The vice president, Dr. Edward Smith and the entire governing board of the University encouraged me a lot.

My sincere love and thanks go to my brother and friend Dr. Gregory Gerrie who invested so much in me. The book you gave me was very helpful.

Meeting Dr. H. Norman Wright was a great inspiration. I treasure the book you gave me, "Crisis And Trauma Counseling."

I am especially thankful to my mentor and father-in-ministry Dr. John Akpami, who had long desired to see this book. You are a father indeed.

To every member of my congregation, I say thank you. My joy is that some of you were recipients of those great testimonies shared in this book. You provided the platform for my ministry. I love you all.

I am also indebted to my brother and friend in ministry, Rev. & Mrs. Tunde J. Spencer, Counsellor for Political Affairs, Embassy of Liberia in Abuja. You are the first to tell me about Phoenix University of Theology. Your support made this possible.

My late parents Jeremiah and Eunice Agala, who painted the first picture I saw about marriage. They left in my mind a positive impression about marriage. They taught me to always look up when seeking for marital solutions, explaining that solutions gotten elsewhere are usually temporal. I am grateful for the godly upbringing.

May I use this opportunity to also thank all my social media and WhatsApp Friends for all your postings. I found some of the stories from unknown authors relevant.

Finally, may all glory, and all honour be ascribed unto our Lord Jesus Christ to whom I owe my existence forever and ever, Amen.

INTRODUCTION

Hello Families

Professionals the world over are collating and analyzing information about the family. They are looking for solutions to the problems faced by the family. One can easily lose count at all the studies that have been done on families.

The problems faced by families vary depending on their age, their status and the culture (society) in which they live.

Poor families in India have different problems from middle-class families in England.

However, both families face similar issues when one examines the tensions between husband and wife, and parents and children.

The Christian family around the world is not immune from these problems and challenges.

It sometimes seems that Christian homes are hit the worst. The indices are clear. The devil has identified the Christian homes as his number one enemy.

He comes up with new strategies on how he can destroy man, God's greatest creation. Because man is created in the image and likeness of God, our enemy satan wants to destroy us.

In the beginning, satan tempted Adam, who then blamed it all upon Eve his wife and silently indicted God the Giver.

Genesis 3:11-13. Eve pointed at the serpent indicting her husband, Adam. This is the point where we all missed it.

The being who should be accused first and receive the blame became the last. And today when family folks realize who their true enemy is, they are left with the damages.

Day after day, family folks keep blaming and fighting one another. The devil is never recognized as the enemy behind the scene. They may realize that at the end of the fight. That is like a man fighting with his eyes closed. You are sure to waste your blows on the wrong target – the innocent.

This book intends to unmask the enemy responsible for this havoc.

Like any other medical condition, an appropriate diagnosis is necessary for identifying the problem, suggesting a solution and a cure and recovery that is permanent. Hence the choice of the title *THE FAMILY CLINIC*.

Here, most of those smoking firebrand issues in homes are brought to light, and the enemy behind them exposed as the root cause.

Once the source of the problem is understood, a solution for most family maladies can be prescribed.

CHAPTER 1

HOW IT ALL STARTED

Going back to the garden, in **Genesis 1:26-30** we read:

Then God said, "Let Us make man in Our image, according to Our likeness; and let them rule over the fish of the sea and over the birds of the sky and over the cattle and over all the earth, and over every creeping thing that creeps on the earth."

27 God created man in His own image, in the image of God He created him; male and female He created them.

28 God blessed them; and God said to them, "Be fruitful and multiply, and fill the earth, and subdue it; and rule over the fish of the sea and over the birds of the sky and over every living thing that moves on the earth."

29 Then God said, "Behold, I have given you every plant yielding seed that is on the surface of all the

earth, and every tree which has fruit yielding seed; it shall be food for you;

30 and to every beast of the earth and to every bird of the sky and to everything that moves on the earth which has life, I have given every green plant for food"; and it was so.

Satan sensed a royal rivalry and observed that God was coming up with another plan too dangerous for his survival.

Satan Fired

"Let us make man in our image" was like a sack of letters too heavy for him to handle. He knows that God does not throw words about. Every word that proceedeth out of His mouth must come to pass.

Isaiah 55:11 "So will My word be which goes forth from My mouth; it will not return to Me empty, without accomplishing what I desire, and without succeeding in the matter for which I sent it"

This was like your boss advertising your current position in your presence.

At this point, you don't need a seer to tell you that your service is no longer required. A plan 'B' will be critical.

Before now, satan had been having a field day. The world was a consolation for him after he was driven out of heaven. He started parading himself as the man in charge here. He thought God had forever abandoned the world because of its pollution.

As though that was not enough. Still, in his devastated condition satan heard God say "... and let them have "DOMINION."

It was like a canister of tear gas fired by the Lord at a close range. Satan was confused and devastated. He saw that he was no more the one in charge of the worldly domain. God handed over authority to the man.

Under this new arrangement, satan and his fallen angels are to take orders from this new being called MAN.

But having tasted power and authority in heaven, the devil vowed never to be a subject to any man in a territory that he considered his domain. This was how the enmity with man began.

Thereafter, satan sees every man, every family, every child of God as an imposter. This was God's arrangement and not necessarily the man's fault, though the man later played into satans hand at when man disobeyed.

The enemy knows that God does not have man as a permanent friend. You remain His friend as long as you remain obedient to His words and instructions.

Satan must have said to himself "I think I know how to stop this nonsense." He quickly came up with a disobedient package which he offered to Eve.

Beloved, what looked like a promo-pack ended up destroying the relationship between God and Man. This brought about shame, reproach, and the passing of blame and even death.

Satan's Happiest Moment - THE FALL

The strategy worked well. satan and his angels watched Adam and his wife struggling to cover up their shame with an apron of leaves. Driven out of the garden by the angel, they blamed themselves and even God for their failure. They were forced to leave the garden watered by God, to fend for themselves. Their eyes were only opened to evil, and they went into hiding.

No more free food. No more beautiful and quiet environment. Animals were no longer friendly. They lived in fear and uncertainty, and the struggling started. The man should from henceforth be responsible.

More celebration for satan when God even cursed the ground for their sake. This was setting the stage for real-time hardship. Favour was withdrawn for labour. Life became "out of thy sweat" what can be harder than that for the first family on earth.

They had no example to follow. No marriage counselor to help. They were examples only to themselves. The only visitor in the garden was the devil.

"Be fruitful and multiply" was not going to be painless anymore. Replenishing the earth became life-threatening to the female folks. This disobedience was the genesis of all today's family problems.

The Disappointment

Well, hope was not lost. While the devil and his angels were busy celebrating the defeat of Mr. and Mrs. Adam, God surprisingly killed an animal and used the skin instead of leaves for their covering. God changed their apron of shame to an apron of glory. Wow!!! The first leather material for a couple who were wearing leaves only minutes ago.

This is exactly what God will do to any shameful and hopeless conditions around your marriage. God has not written you off. Get ready for an apron of glory in place of that apron of shame. God went as far as shedding the first blood to cover their shame.

Friends, the death and the blood of Jesus are more than enough to cover any kind of disgrace, reproach and shame the enemy have inflicted on your family. Cheer up and get ready to amend things. Because God does not abandon His own.

Satan was shocked that Adam's case was handled differently. God was not letting go of Adam and his wife. He had a redemptive plan in mind while the enmity continues between satan and God's families until satan's head is finally bruised and crushed.

The action of God was in the interest of the family. God drove them out of the garden, not to destroy them, but as a temporary measure in order not to make their deplorable condition permanent before His son Jesus comes to restore them.

"...Lest he put forth and take also of the tree of life, and eat and live forever" **(Genesis 3:22)** in that condition.

As you can see, the devil is the real culprit and not your wife, children, or your husband. This understanding will go a long way in making families realize who their real enemy is.

The gospel of Matthew will introduce a united front in the fight. The result will be the benefit of co-operate engagement where we are to determine the outcome "...bound and it will be bound loose, and it will be loosed in heaven." **(Matthew16:19)**

CHAPTER 2

BEFORE YOU SAY YES

Recently I saw a Whatsapp message (Author unknown) sharing a similar opinion with some singles. This shows how concerned God is about our relationship. The truth is that commitment has two sides, and so does its consequences.

Every second, thousands of foundations are being laid with the holy intention of building marriage towers. Proposals upon proposals. But the question remains, how many of them stand out as a magnificent tower that the designer (God) wants to see.

Marriage Towers

The editors of the Encyclopedia Britannica (www.Britannica.com), defined a tower as any structure that is relatively tall in proportion to the dimensions of its base. They are built for different purposes such as Military, Communications and so on. In this discussion, marriages are seen as one of those towers. And like the tower of Babel, marriage towers can be built to heaven if there is effective communication.

Gen.11:4-7

"And they said, Go to, let us build us a city and a tower, whose top may reach unto heaven; and let us make us a name, lest we be scattered abroad upon the face of the whole earth.

5 And the LORD came down to see the city and the tower, which the children of men builded.

6 And the LORD said, Behold, the people is one, and they have all one language; and this they begin to do: and now nothing will be restrained from them, which they have imagined to do.

7 Go to, let us go down, and there confound their language, that they may not understand one another's speech."

Marriage towers are not just mere makeshift structures. They are something very strong and solid. The Lord gave us an excellent illustration in the book of Luke.

Luke 14:28-30

"28 For which of you, intending to build a **TOWER**, sitteth not down first, and counteth the cost, whether he have sufficient to finish it?

29 Lest haply, after he hath laid the foundation, and is not able to finish it, all that behold it begin to mock him,

30 Saying, 'This man began to build, and was not able to finish.'"

According to the Advanced English Dictionary, a makeshift structure refers to "anything done or made using whatever is available." But such a casual statement does not apply to a tower.

A tower, therefore, refers to a very strong tall structure occupying a commanding position. This is the exact position God wants every family to occupy.

There are many kinds of towers today. eg the Aviation Tower for aviation purposes and Military Surveillance Towers for military purposes. Others are Telecommunications Towers, Tourist Towers and so on.

These are not makeshift structures. They are not the common structures you find in your streets. Not a project that can be financed from your back pocket. You must definitely sit down to count the cost as Jesus said in **Luke 14:28** "For which of you, intending to build a tower, sitteth not down first, and counteth the cost, whether he have sufficient to finish it?"

As you can see, marriage is not a dance for feeble feet. It requires you sitting down with the Lord who is both the Architect and the Quality Surveyor of marriage institutions. As the Master Designer, only He can supervise your marriage with great precision according to His Divine purpose. He knows the future; He knows the purpose and has limitless resources.

Every tower has a purpose. So also is your marriage. There is a purpose for every family on earth.

Beloved, lay a good foundation for your home. Don't join yourself with **any person** in the name of relationship because **the** destinies are not the same. Homes need to be constituted according to destiny and purpose, not according to wishes and desires.

As you read on, you will agree that man is the most complicated among homo sapiens.

Jeremiah 17:9 says "The heart is deceitful above all things, and desperately wicked: who can know it?" But the good news is, that the more you see God clearly, the more plainly and demystified the man becomes. So you don't have to be a trained investigator or a detective before starting a relationship. The truth is that God can help you answer any question about any human being

As you sit with the Lord to count the cost, the following questions may help you in your marriage analysis.

1. Who is this person and what are their personality traits?

According to Tim LaHaye, in his book *Why You Act The Way You Do*, writes "Temperament influences everything you do—from sleep habits to study habits to eating style to the way you get along with other people." Though the Bible does not recommend a college degree in Psychology before getting married to anyone, basic knowledge about the spouse to be is in order.

2. Does he or she love God?

This is what determines the future outlook of any home. Ask yourself, "Is it possible for someone who does not love God to love me in marriage?" I don't know what your answer is. But mine is NO. In fact, it is impossible. The Bible says in **1 John 4:21** "And this commandment have we from Him, that he who loveth God love his brother also." This means, no love for God: no love for you. Human beings are naturally selfish. It will be strange and out of order for someone who does not care how God feels about his actions to love and **care** for his wife. Every genuine horizontal relationship is as a result of a healthy vertical relationship with God. **Love is the nature of God, so anyone who is less than God cannot manifest it.**

3. Does he or she submit to God and God's authority?

The question is "Can I survive a man or woman whom God cannot restrain?" Such a person is a ready vessel in the hand of satan—too dangerous with whom to associate. Satan can sponsor irrational decisions at will, and no one can stop him or call satan to order.

Ephesians 5:21 "Submitting yourselves one to another in the fear of God." This scripture is the kingdom recipe for world peace. This is the key for a lifetime harmony in the home.

Can you imagine a world where we submit ourselves one to another in the fear of God? Such a world does not exist you will say. Yes, but we can create this world in our homes.

1 Cor.16:15-17 "I beseech you, brethren, (ye know the house of Stephanas, that it is the first fruits of Achaia, and that they have addicted themselves to the ministry of the saints,) That ye submit yourselves unto such, and to every one that helpeth with us, and laboureth."

The Stephenas family is indeed a family to emulate. The Apostle Paul asks us to submit to such. Why? Because they first submitted themselves to God. Peace reigns in any relationship where this is practiced.

Heb. 13:17 "Obey them that have the rule over you, and submit yourselves: for they watch for your souls, as they that must give account, that they may do it with joy, and not with grief: for that is unprofitable for you."

4. Where does he or she want to live?

This question may sound very simple and insignificant. But it has the ability to bring joy or perpetual regrets to the family depending on what the answer is. Some men are naturally country people. City living irritates them. Such places are too busy for their liking. The architectural masterpieces in the downtown do not appeal to their eyes. They are rather attracted to those simple huts surrounded by farm

22

crops. They are happy when they see livestock grazing freely in the neighborhood.

For others, passing a night in such a place is hellish. They wonder why human beings should live in such places. They see it as homes for wild animals. And if anything human lives there, they must be the poorest of the poor. So if you are a city person, you need to stay away from such a person. Otherwise, you will live the rest of your lives in frustration. The problem starts with separation and ends in divorce. Very few people adapt over the years. **The problem here is not the person but the place.**

5. What are his or her beliefs in life? Do I have contrary beliefs?

The Advanced English Dictionary defined beliefs as "Any cognitive content held as true or a vague idea in which confidence is placed." So, in order to avoid a conflict-ridden relationship, efforts should be made to discover those beliefs. Those '**cognitive contents**' including those '**vague ideas**' he/she has held onto all these years. Those beliefs may have become part of them. Any attempt to change them will be strongly resisted. Conflict begins whenever one of the partners insists on a change.

A popular adage in Eastern Nigeria says that "**Changing a man's beliefs is like teaching a pig to sing**. **It wearies the man and annoys the pig.**" This process is an exercise in futility.

A similar scenario exists at conversion. A lot of people believe they can convert their partners after they are married. But experience shows it **rarely** works out. In **Jeremiah 17:9** the Bible says "The heart is deceitful above all things, and desperately wicked: who can know it?"

Who can know it my brothers and sisters?

6. What are his or her ideas about marriage? Are they parochial and selfish?

Different people have different ideas about marriage. Some good people could have bad ideas about marriage and vice versa. Yes, his/her financial ideas are perfect. He has excellent academic records and is even very religious. But his views about marriage are awful. This could be due to upbringing, poor family values, and the norms around him.

Other men are staunch traditionalists, and that's how they run their homes. They don't bother about what the law and the Scripture says. The only thing they tell their spouse is what their forefathers said women should or shouldn't do. They say women must not have more money than their husbands. Women must not have a say in the number of children the family should have. From the beginning of the relationship to the end, it is "Women 'must' and women 'must not.'"

Some other traditions even forbid the men to tell their wives everything about themselves. Women are not supposed to know what their husbands earn. Worse still, some traditions believe that it is the woman who should work and feed the family while the husband attends to crucial traditional issues in the neighborhood.

Some folks have made marriage look like another version of slavery. However, in the case of marriage, the consent of the 'slave' person is solved by asking for her hand in marriage. Whoever then says yes to such a person should be ready for lifelong modern-day slavery in a grand style.

Some years back, I attended the wedding of one Apostle who married one of our faithful sisters in the Lord. A day after the wedding, he came up with what he called his own "**Ten Commandments for Marriage.**" and the commandments were ten in number. All the ten were for the wife to obey and none for the Apostle.

Here were some of the Apostle's Ten Commandments:
  § She must wake up daily at 4 am unfailingly
  § Return to the bed with a cup of tea to wake the Apostle. She must make the presentation on her knees.
  § She must never come to bed clothed.

To hell with the Apostle, some of you will say. Yes, you are right. But more terrible things than these are happening in many relationships today. This is just one scenario.

Well, for this Apostle, this was an ideal marriage.

7. How does he or she see money?

An English adage says, "Money separates the best of friends," and I will want to add "especially where one of them has love for it."

1 John 2:15 & 16 "Love not the world, neither the things that are in the world. If any man love the world, the love of the Father is not in him.

16 For all that is in the world, the lust of the flesh, and the lust of the eyes, and the pride of life, is not of the Father, but is of the world."

1 Timothy 6:10 "For the **love** of money is the root of all evil: which while some coveted after, they have erred from the faith, and pierced themselves through with many sorrows."

This Scripture seems to be more relevant in our generation than when it was written. Today, when you think of what money can do, you will be tempted to rewrite this Scripture. Even now, some people argue to the contrary. But what is written is written.

To love money means allowing money have you, instead of you having money. A lot of people are controlled by money. Money becomes the master **whom** they serve. That is why they can break God's law to get it. When you break God's law to get money, at that time, you have chosen a new master to obey. The new master has a beautiful name called MAMMON.

Luke. 16:13 "No servant can serve two masters: for either, he will hate the one, and love the other;

or else he will hold to the one and despise the other. Ye cannot serve God and mammon."

Yes, this is the Scripture. The only option you have is to serve God or mammon and not God and mammon. **Mammon must be a servant, not a master.**

In Luke 16:10-11 mammon (money) must not just be a servant, but the least of the servants. "He that is faithful in that which is least is faithful also in much: and he that is unjust in the least is unjust also in much. If therefore ye have not been faithful in the unrighteous mammon, who will commit to your trust the true riches?"

Other Things To Note

Some people have a very strong parental tie. They believe they cannot make meaningful decisions without the parents' assistance. Most women can't tolerate that. Some men become obsessed and even go to their parents' graveyards to inquire of them. They emphasize what their late mother told them in a dream and how it must be obeyed. Because for them, it is superior to anyone else's ideas. They mortgage their rights and liberty in spite of numerous state laws that seemed to liberate them with rights of independence. Not too many women will like to spend a night with such a person.

Gen2:24 "Therefore shall a man leave his father and his mother, and shall cleave unto his wife: and they shall be one flesh."

To me, this is the real test of manhood. Any man who cannot leave his father and his mother should not think of husbanding any woman until he is weaned from his parents.

You must also be conscious of how he talks to people. Is he rude and impatient with people, especially the waiters, taxi drivers, etc? You may decide to tolerate from the beginning such weak traits, possibly praying for him without complaining. But when he lies to people, he will need to repent and get a new birth. No relationship can ever thrive under a lie.

You may need to check on your views whether they are polarized. Looking at his goals in life, and putting them side by side with the things you cherish in life, do they seem to be going in opposite directions? If they are, then you have a potential conflict at hand. But this can be resolved with the principle of give and take. The idea is to bring the different views together and realign them into one common goal that will be acceptable and profitable for the entire family.

CHAPTER 3

DO NOT LIE

TO YOUR SPOUSE OR ANYONE ELSE: OTHERWISE, YOU WILL BE ON YOUR WAY TO HELL

Don't Make The Devil Your Teacher

I had an uncle who was a husband to many wives. He told me that those who discovered and introduced lies to this world shall live long. He said his wives would have killed him long ago, were it not for the lies he told them. He believed that women are happier with lies than with truth. He called it a tested instrument for a happy home.

While he was yet speaking, two of his wives arrived on the scene with their shopping bags, heading to the local market for routine shopping for the family.

Before they arrived, he told me to watch and see how he would handle them. He said this was a pure crisis situation as he had no money in his pocket.

"Onyekachi, (as he usually called me) the only thing that will save me now is a good lie," he said, motioning in the direction of the women.

Of a truth, the women were not looking friendly at all. You could see intolerance written all over them. They were not willing to take no for an answer. But their countenance did not ruffle him in any way. He was familiar with their words and actions.

My uncle first calmed them down with a lie before listening to their request. They presented their demands while standing. I watched with keen interest. As a young man yet to be married, it was a case study for me. I had planned to use this method in the future when I got married. However, I never knew that I was taking tutorials from the devil who wanted to infuse the spirit of lying into my life.

Guess what? The strategy worked. He dismissed them with what he called 'a good lie.' I was shocked that the wives believed him and went away happy. What saved me from implementing such evil lectures was the privilege of knowing the Lord long before my uncle's tutorials.

What Is A Lie?

According to Microsoft Encarta Premium 2009, to lie means "to say something that is not true in a conscious effort to deceive somebody."

This includes all false impressions, tricks, flattering, withholding information, etc. When you live like this, you are said to be dishonest.

From the little experiences I gathered in my twenty-four years of marriage; I discovered that good impressions improve a relationship. What kills a relationship is false impressions. It makes the people live a fake life. Falsehood breeds distrust and misgivings, therefore setting the stage for suspicion. This is never sustainable. Because it takes a lot to maintain a lie for long, the parties end up becoming suspect of each other throughout the marriage relationship, if nothing is done to change this method of interaction.

Versions Of Lies

Which version of lies do you manifest? Today, lying has become more popular than the truth. People only tell the truth if there is no consequence. They say YES or NO depending on the consequences. I am going to be pretty hard on this topic because, for a lot of people, the peace in their relationship and their ultimate destiny with God depends on what they do with this understanding about a lie.

Every passing day, the devil launches his campaign of falsehoods; making people believe this is the present day way of wisdom. These lies are presented under different topics such as Diplomacy, Smartness, Administrative Politeness, and some are branded as mere political speeches. It is common in these days for people to err and look for sweet sounding words to Christianize the blunder. People lie, cheat, deprive and defraud others, and the devil will tell them they are just being smart.

Each formal and informal sector has their own terminology. They are taught to speak politely to people without divulging the truth. They call it "administrative politeness." Some call it "marketing." Others call it "PR - public relations." The politicians call it "a political speech."

God calls it lying.

You may have different opinions about this, but God is no respecter of persons, organizations, or nations as we can see in the following scriptures.

Acts 10:34-35

"Then Peter opened his mouth, and said, 'Of a truth, I perceive that God is no respecter of persons:

35 But in every nation, he that feareth him, and worketh righteousness, is accepted with him.'"

The above Scripture seems not to recognize World Powers, Third World Countries, Developed and Undeveloped Countries. God is saying, no matter the country of your origin, if you fear Him and live a righteous life, you will be accepted.

Righteousness does not respond to color, height or size.

Diplomacy

According to the Advanced English Dictionary; *diplomacy* refers to a subtle and skillful handling of a situation. You may not have anything against this definition until you pay attention to the word *"subtle"*

The same Advanced English Dictionary defined the

word "*subtle*" to mean "difficult to detect or grasp by the mind" that is, being elusive in speech and character.

In **Gen. 3:1a** the Bible says "Now the serpent was more **subtle** than any beast of the field which the LORD God had made." It is the nature of Satan to be subtle, deceptive and elusive. It is not in your character as a child of God. And more also because you don't have the nature of Satan but the new nature of God.

Today we see nations relate to each other in manner elusive in all aspects of international relations. All in the name of diplomacy. They meditate over other Nations basically for their own interests. They proffer solutions, grants, aid and other humanitarian packages all wrapped around selfish interests in a manner difficult to detect or grasp by the minds of the recipients. This is an outright falsehood.

Some families run their homes with the same principles. I attended seminars where men are taught to use diplomacy in dealing with their wives. This is not different from my uncle's lesson on lying. This is not the same as relating to your wife with understanding. Diplomacy refers to actions with hidden motives. This is a version of lying. So we must count God out of such actions. God does not operate diplomatically.

God Is Straightforward

John 1:17 says "Every good and every perfect gift is from above, and cometh down from the Father of Lights, with whom is no variableness, neither shadow of turning."

God is straightforward in all His dealings. My father, in the faith, Dr. John Akpami said that "God does not tantalize anybody with words. He doesn't just speak to make anyone happy. He doesn't present dark speeches."

James 5:12b puts it this way from Good News Translation . "...say only 'Yes' when you mean yes and 'No' when you mean no, and then you will not come under God's judgment."

Brethren what I say to you, I say to myself. It is God addressing His people on this subtle, controversial but crucial matter. Let us develop a bitter hatred for lying the same way we hate murder, idolatry and other vices.

Don't Categorize Sin

Leviticus 19:11 "Ye shall not steal, neither deal falsely, neither lie one to another. In this single sentence in Leviticus, the same lawgiver who said ye shall not steal also told us not to lie or deal falsely one to another."

In as much as you wouldn't steal when "necessary," so also, don't listen to the devil when he tells you that you are permitted to lie when necessary. It is like saying I only commit sin when necessary. Someone ironically said people tell lies to avoid committing a much bigger sin. ***Friend, at no time,*** *is lying necessary. The truth is that God knows how to remove from you those circumstances that can put you in a tight corner those lying corners.*

Lying is clearly stated among the kingdom contrabands.

Revelations 21:8 "But the fearful, and unbelieving, and the abominable, and murderers, and whoremongers, and sorcerers, and idolaters, and all liars, shall have their part in the lake which burneth with fire and brimstone: which is the second death."

Now look at the list closely again:

1. The Fearful
2. The Unbelieving
3. The Abominable
4. Murderers
5. Whoremongers
6. Sorcerers
7. Idolatry
8. And All Liars.

Permit me to say that though number eight is last, it is never the least. Beloved, this list is inexhaustive. The list continues in other scriptures such as

Galatians 5:19-21

"Now the works of the flesh are manifest, which are these; adultery, fornication, uncleanness, lasciviousness,

20 Idolatry, witchcraft, hatred, variance, emulations, wrath, strife, seditions, heresies,

21 Envyings, murders, drunkenness, revellings, and such like: of the which I tell you before, as I have

also told you in time past, that they which do such things shall not inherit the kingdom of God."

The devil is doing everything to expunge number eight from the list. Seeing that this was not possible for him, he makes people believe that, since it is the last, it is, therefore, the least. Hence the categorization of sin.

James 2:10

"For whosoever shall keep the whole law, and yet offend in one point, he is guilty of all."

This is why we must not categorize sin.

The Purpose Of Every Lie

The purpose of every lie is to deceive, and whoever deceives is called a deceiver. I am sure you know whose name that is; yeah **satan** for sure. It doesn't sound like your name.

Friends, the devil has done everything to legalize lies in spite of their devastating consequences. He designed the first day of April as a day when lies can freely be told.

Wake up child of God and wise up. The devil is trying to make a fool of us by making the sin of lying look very insignificant. satan knows very well that God said, "no liar will have a part in His kingdom." So with the sin of lying, he is sure of taking more people to hell than that of killing, adultery and so on. Do you see the game plan?

Unfortunately, most Church sermons are not usually

on this subject. I have hardly come across any man of God who comes up to the pulpit announcing to the people that today my topic is "THOU SHALL NOT LIE."

Such topics are not popular anymore. It is not amongst the sermon topics preachers describe as "Message For The Now." It doesn't attract the applause of the people who have developed itching ears.

What you have as a result is, brethren, lying at will, as if there is no consequence associated. People do all manner of things and deny ever doing such things.

They keep a lady for fornication and tell the neighbors she is his younger sister looking for a job. Some others have wives and children elsewhere, but when they meet another woman, they swear an oath that there is no other person in their lives, never. Because of this, many marriages are solemnized in deceit and falsehood, causing confusion everywhere. The fear of God has disappeared in our generation. Lies are told right inside the church hall with impunity. Lies are told in the name of testimonies. Ministers fake miracles. They want to impress the people. Even when ushers awake those found sleeping during the sermon, they vehemently deny ever sleeping.

Parents lie to their children and even make them tell lies too. The children are beaten when they tell the truth against their parents.

I escorted a friend of mine to a family I respected very well. He repaired their television set and now wanted to collect his money. The homeowner crawled under the bed and told his four-year-old son to tell us he wasn't home. When we asked, the son told us that daddy said he wasn't around.

He gestured with his hands, pointed under the bed with his index finger and said: "Uncle come and see Daddy's legs under the bed."

Shame on those parents who had made lying a way of life. Only God knows what will happen to the child. Will he receive the beating of his life? Why? Because he is expected to defend his parents with a lie. To the parents, this boy is not wise and intelligent. Poor innocent boy. The same parents would want the child to tell them the truth about his homework, who came to the house in their absence, and what they know about the missing money and so on and so forth.

In some African communities, you dare not tell the truth about a masquerade, a deity or reveal a community lie which has been upheld as a truth for centuries. They formulate lies about their history. To them, what is truth is only that which is in their favour.

Some cultures don't even believe a man should tell his wife everything about himself. This includes his salary, his properties, and some of his investments. He could decide not to tell the wife about his previous relationship, and it is all acceptable. If these lead to a conflict, the wife will be told to remember he is a man. The church is filled with traditionalists whose heart is far away from God. Stand with the truth and don't go their way. Learn from Jesus encounter with such people in the past.

Matthew 15:1; 2a; 3; 6b; 7&8

1 "Then came to Jesus scribes and Pharisees, which were of Jerusalem, saying,

2a Why do thy disciples transgress the tradition of the elders?.

3 But he answered and said unto them, Why do ye also transgress the commandment of God by your tradition?

6b Thus have ye made the commandment of God of none effect by your tradition.

7 Ye hypocrites, well did Esaias prophesy of you, saying,

8 This people draweth nigh unto me with their mouth, and honoureth me with their lips; but their heart is far from me."

Jesus called them hypocrites. What was their offense? They exalted the tradition of men above the commandment of God. God's tradition is embedded in His commandment. Determine today to run the affairs of your family on God's Word which is called the Truth. Brethren think about these things and ask God to help you take a stand with the truth and have nothing to do with lying forever. When you do this, you will be loved by God, and the devil will divorce you in a hurry.

Paul said in **Romans 6:1-2** "What shall we say then? Shall we continue in sin, that grace may abound? 2 God forbid. How shall we, that are dead to sin, live any longer therein?"

Just imagine a world without lying. You would have gotten a glimpse of heaven in your imagination.

Here is what God Said:

Proverbs 12:22 "Lying lips are an abomination to the LORD: but they that deal truly are his delight."

According to Merriam Webster dictionary, abomination means "extreme disgust and hatred."

Beloved, I want to suggest you begin to see lying the same way God sees it. Nothing short of "extreme disgust and hatred." This is the only way we can save our soul from eternal damnation.

Friends, before you claim and celebrate **Psalms 23:6** which says "Surely goodness and mercy shall follow me all the days of my life: and I will dwell in the house of the LORD forever," carefully consider **Psalms 101:7** "He that worketh deceit shall not dwell within my house: he that telleth lies shall not tarry in my sight."

God is saying that **Psalms 101:7** is not for him that worketh deceit. The grammar is not ambiguous. God in plain terms said He will send you packing out of His house. God cannot tolerate the sight of a liar. It means you will be separated from Goodness and from Mercy. What a life.

Proverbs 6:16-17 "These six things doth the LORD hate: yea, seven are an abomination unto him:

17 A proud look, a lying tongue, and hands that shed innocent blood."

A lying tongue is on the list of the seven things forbidden by the Lord.

The Lord made a very fearful statement in **John 8:44c.**

John 8:44c "Ye are of your father the devil, and the lusts of your father ye will do. He was a murderer from the beginning, and abode not in the truth, because there is no truth in him. When he speaketh a lie, he speaketh of his own: for he is a liar, and the father of it."

God publicly announced to us who the father of all liars is. His name is satan. He is first a liar and the father of them. ***The only truth about the devil is that he is a liar.***

Proverbs 13:5 "A righteous man hateth lying: but a wicked man is loathsome, and cometh to shame."

Ephesians 4:25 "Wherefore putting away lying, speak every man truth with his neighbour: for we are members one of another."

Ephesians 4:29 "Let no corrupt communication proceed out of your mouth, but that which is good to the use of edifying, that it may minister grace unto the hearers."

Psalms 58:3 "The wicked are estranged from the womb: they go astray as soon as they be born, speaking lies. The World English Bible (WEB) puts it this way "The wicked go astray from the womb. They are wayward as soon as they are born, speaking lies."

Psalms 116:11 "I said in my haste, All men are liars."

Acts 5: 3-4 "But Peter said, Ananias, why hath Satan filled thine heart to lie to the Holy Ghost, and to keep back part of the price of the land?

4 Whiles it remained, was it not thine own? And

after it was sold, was it not in thine own power? Why hast thou conceived this thing in thine heart? Thou hast not lied unto men, but unto God."

Colossians 3:9 "Lie not one to another, seeing that ye have put off the old man with his deeds."

James 5:12 "But above all things, my brethren, swear not, neither by heaven, neither by the earth, neither by any other oath: but let your yea be yea; and your nay, nay; lest ye fall into condemnation."

Proverbs 30:7-8 "I ask you, God, to let me have two things before I die; keep me from lying, and let me be neither rich nor poor. So give me only as much food as I need." (GNT)

Lying is sponsored by a spirit. This is why we should do more radical things than just wishing we will never lie again.

Let us pray this prayer together.
1. Holy Father, I command the lying spirit to leave in the name of the Lord Jesus Christ. From henceforth, I cease to speak under your influence.
2. Father, I purify my tongue with the precious blood of the Lord Jesus Christ.
3. In the Name of Jesus, I dedicate my tongue to the truth and nothing but the truth.

Lord thank you for saving my family and me from the spirit of lying in Jesus name Amen.

CHAPTER 4

MALICE BETWEEN HUSBAND AND WIFE

A friend of mine posted this story on Whatsapp messenger. This happened to someone he knows. The story was titled *"I Killed My Wife."* This was posted as a warning to those couples still dealing with this destructive and defective behavioral signet called malice. The story is paraphrased below.

The brother and his wife were both committed members of a vibrant church. They occupied different leadership positions in the church.

One day, a quarrel erupted between them, and this lingered unresolved for three days. On the third Sunday, they both went to Church in that unhealthy condition.

At the end of the service, the husband drove home with the kids who were hungry and wanted to get home quickly for their meals. The children went to sleep immediately after the late lunch leaving their father in the living room watching some television programs.

Usually, the family attended church services using only one car. But this fateful Sunday, husband and wife went to church in different cars. This was necessary because they were not on speaking terms.

The wife stayed after the service for a meeting with the women. She was the women's fellowship leader. Due to an asthmatic condition, she usually carried an inhaler. Unfortunately, that very Sunday she left for the church service and forgot her inhaler. Her husband who was her partner in malice cared less and never bothered about the forgotten inhaler even though he saw she had left it behind.

At the end of the women's meeting, she started driving home alone. On the way, in fact, very close to her home, the enemy struck with an asthmatic attack and behold, she had no inhaler.

Under attack, she made a desperate call to her husband for the inhaler. Her life was on the line. Each time her husband saw her call, he ignored it, keeping his knees together with his eyes on the television. She called repeatedly while driving until she made it into her compound with her last breath. Even her last call from inside the compound was ignored.

She helplessly gave up the ghost and died. The strange manner her car was parked attracted attention, but no one suspected anything.

Her husband, who had been looking out the window of the parlor, now wanted to go out. He told the gate man to inform his wife to move the car. The gateman replied that madam was sleeping. On coming down, probably to shout at her, the husband discovered that his wife was dead.

Knowing what had happened, he started shouting, "I KILLED MY WIFE; I KILLED MY WIFE."

What a sad story. Who knew that malice could lead to such a tragic end? How I wish that the end of every malicious behavior could be known right at its inception.

The songwriter, Charlotte Elliott, (1836) in her song 'Christian seek not yet repose' wrote in one of the stanzas.

Principalities and Powers,
Mustering their unseen array,
Wait for thy unguarded hours:
Watch and Pray.
In stanza four she added that
"Ambushed lies the evil one, Watch and Pray."

This is an ambush against the Christian home. It can happen to anyone unless we watch and pray. The devil waits for unguarded hours to strike. He takes advantage of our weaknesses.

What Is Malice?

The complete *Christian Dictionary For Home And School*, 1990, 1992 by the International Bible Society, defines malice "as the desire to hurt other people or to see others suffer."

Do you desire to hurt other people and to see them suffer? Without further investigation, we realize that the devil is the sponsor of every form of malice. This is not part of our character as children of God. satan is the scriptwriter of every malice. He is malicious by nature. His desire is to hurt people and watch them suffer. He has a bitter hatred for humans. He likes to instigate bad behavior, creating a platform for their self-destruction.

In the classification of offenses, malice is believed to be a legal term though also applicable in other fields of life. According to Taniya Prusty's online publication, there is malice-in-fact and malice-in-law. He tried explaining the difference between the two terminologies as shown below.

Malice-in-fact

1. Malice-in-fact is an act done with ill will towards an individual.
2. Malice-in-fact depends upon motive.
3. Malice-in-fact means ill-will or any vindictive motive against a person.
4. It is also known as "Actual malice" or "Express malice."

Malice-in-law.

1. Malice-in-law means an act done wrongfully and without reasonable and probable cause.
2. Malice-in-law depends upon knowledge.
3. Malice-in-law means the concurrence of mind with a wrongful act done without just cause or excuse.
4. Malice-in-law is also known as "Implied Malice."   Source: *1.bp.blogspot.com.*

Humans can sometimes be outrightly malicious. The devil uses them to unleash wickedness and horror against humanity. The incidences abound in many quarters. It is not news to hear that a man stabbed his pregnant wife to death. Children are used for disgusting acts in secret cults.

You are wondering if a Christian can be involved in such acts. The truth is that no true child of God will do that. But, unfortunately, some of these people find themselves in some churches for whatever reason.

Gerald N. Hill and Kathleen T. Hill, (1981-2005) talking about "**Expressed Malice**" said that:

"Often the mean nature of the act itself implies malice, without the party saying "I did it because I was mad at him, and I hated him," which will be expressed malice. Here we know who is in operation. Your guess is right, the devil. He is mean in nature.

It is interesting to note, that long before the human judiciary was instituted, God spoke of malice in His book, the Bible.

St Paul in his First Epistle to the Corinthians declared in 5:6 "Your glorying is not good. Know ye not that a little leaven leaveneth the whole lump?

7 Purge out therefore the old leaven, that ye may be a new lump, as ye are unleavened. For even Christ our Passover is sacrificed for us:

8 Therefore let us keep the feast, not with old leaven, neither with the leaven of malice and wickedness; but with the unleavened bread of sincerity and truth". **1 Corinthians 5:6-8**

The Leaven Of Malice

Malice, when brewed takes time to ferment. It doesn't happen overnight. It starts from simple displeasure to a total breakdown in communication. A little leaven the Bible calls it.

It acts like the baker's yeast. Linda Stanley, in a web publication, declared that: "The main reason yeast is introduced by the baker is for it to serve as a catalyst in the process of fermentation. This is essential in the making of bread. Otherwise, the bread will not rise. What the leavener does, is to feed on the sugar in flour, and expel carbon dioxide in the process" *www.whatscookingamerica.net*

The devil usually is the chief baker. He subtly releases all manners of yeast into sweet relationships. This yeast eats the sugars–the sweetness of that relationship, leaving behind a gas called carbon dioxide in the form of sour relationships and very unpleasant situations. This is contrary to the plan of God for families. God wants the best for us. He is delighted to see us happy. Child of God, never allow the devil to tamper with your marriage dough. The enemy goes about with a lot of "malice-yeast." Don't allow him near your matrimonial dough. He will pollute it.

Some of those simple pollutants include:

Lack of Lovely Compliments

Women tend to keep a compliment register in their minds. The scores are registered during the day: the result of which could be used in favor or against the husband at night. If the man is lucky, his attention could be drawn to the scoreboard. He may be asked to explain why he did not say anything about the makeup combos, the choice of her clothes to the service or party, the color of the handbag, the shoes, the new hairstyle after the salon visit and on and on. The list continues. Some other women will keep the scoreboard to themselves. This is more dangerous than the former. Here the entire relationship sits on a "malice gunpowder."

This is what your four-year-old girl will do, isn't it? Exactly! Pastor. Yes, you are right in your response. But you must realize that as far as lovely compliments are concerned, there is no adult woman. If you are blessed to have your grandparents alive, you will observe that your grandmother in her eighties still crosschecks her looks with the grandpa to be confident. You are wondering why it should be so. My brother, this should not be a research topic for you. The answer is nor far-fetched. She is just configured that way. Behaving otherwise is rather strange.

Someone said, "A man's biggest mistake is giving another man the opportunity to make his woman smile." *www.loveandsayings.com.*

Sometimes, they may not be asking for too much,

a look of admiration and a gentle smile can earn you some marks. Saying nothing at all may be the yeast in the hand of the devil. This can leaven the marriage dough and ruin the entire marriage relationships.

Tone of Voice

A local adage often spoken in my community says: "When a quarrel ends up in a shout, it means the quarreling parties have no more words to exchange." The only time you shout at a woman and go scot-free is if it is a shout of praise. You are permitted to disturb the neighborhood at her arrival. In fact, those encomiums should not be bestowed on her in secret. She feels like the queen mother in the mist of her subjects. You may be required to face some charges if anything on the contrary. This is not peculiar to women. No one hates praise, no matter the tone in which it is presented.

Declining Advances

Declining advances especially sexual advances is a major cause of malice in most homes. I hear many husbands saying "That's it, ride on pastor." Yes, I will ride on, but don't forget that it can come from either of you. Although, more frequently from the female folks. When women do this, they shoot themselves in the foot without knowing it. Women should know that unnecessarily turning down sexual advances is like forcefully quenching a burning candle without minding whose eyes the smoke will irritate.

When this happens, many things come under attack. The first is communication flow. Greetings suddenly become unnecessarily brief. Spouses respond to issues without interest. Sessions of one-word answers begin no matter the length of the questions.

My friend, wake up! Can't you see that the devil is at it again? The yeast is at work. The dough is rising. This is when one must be a man of understanding. Take back your marriage and don't play into the enemy's gallery.

Here is what Apostle Paul said in **1 Corinthians 14:20** "Brethren, be not children in understanding: howbeit in malice be ye children, but in understanding be men."

Too Busy for Each Other

This is one of those things to watch. The devil can subtly use it as yeast to leaven your loaf. Do not spiritualize this issue if you are a minister. The devil has pushed some spouses into certain irrational decisions most of which are irreparable. People do funny things in order to make up. Cases abound where wives have lain with the gatemen or even her driver. House girls also become deputy wives. The devil tells them that all men are the same and they serve the same purpose and give the same satisfaction. Life must go on they say. He tells the man the same thing. I have heard of the wife of a very senior government official reserving a hotel room permanently for her driver solely for the same purpose.

The Apostle Paul stated in: **1 Corinthians 7:2-5**

"Nevertheless, to avoid fornication, let every man have his own wife, and let every woman have her own husband..." To avoid fornication shows us how close infidelity is to any couple. The devil is just waiting for our unguarded hours. So Paul declared in verse three:

"Let the husband render unto the wife due benevolence: and likewise also the wife unto the husband. The wife hath not power of her own body, but the husband: and likewise also the husband hath not power of his own body, but the wife. Defraud ye not one the other, except it be with consent for a time, that ye may give yourselves to fasting and prayer; and come together again, that Satan tempt you not for your incontinency."

So let us not give the devil the opportunity to tempt us.

Issues Under the Carpet

It is important to learn how to sweep issues straight to the garbage bin and not under your carpet. Let the issues be discussed and be disposed of. Don't have an "issue register" at home, whether resolved or unresolved. This is because issues resurrect on their own without much prayer. So bury them far away from your homes. Don't make your heart a dumping ground for fresh and unresolved issues. Your heart is too tender to bear them. Moreover, it is not configured for such things.

Open Rebuke

A lot of people don't really mind being rebuked as long as you don't go public with it. They did something wrong, YES, but you must know how to correct. It is an art. Effort should be made not to go public with rebukes that are offensive.

The first epistle of Paul the Apostle to Timothy explained the ways correction can be affected. Offensive rebukes are what often separates the best of couples.

1 Timothy 5:1 -2 "Rebuke not an elder, but entreat him as a father; and the younger men as brethren; The elder women as mothers; the younger as sisters, with all purity."

No one given a First Timothy 5 treatment will reject that correction. The above method is garnished in love.

There are other instances where open rebuke is inevitable. When offense is committed openly everyone is watching to know what your stand is on the matter. Secret rebuke or correction, in this case, may be interpreted as condoning evil.

The Psalmist in **Psalm 6:1** introduces another side

to it. He said, "O LORD, rebuke me not in thine anger, neither chasten me in thy hot displeasure."

The above scripture determines what the outcome will be. So without the wisdom of God, open rebuke becomes a leavener in the hand of the devil.

Disrespect

"Respect is reciprocal," an English adage said. The boss should be seen as the boss. From creation, God made the man the boss, and in marriage, he made him the head. The female folks don't need to fight this position. It will be a needless fight. Failure to understand this will lead to endless rancor on the home front, as the man will never be willing to give up his position of authority. The man, however, must realize he is only the boss and not a god. Any leader who is disrespectful to his followers will never succeed. The wife must accept her role as the deputy boss. Or the boss pro tempore in the absence of her husband. She must not be arrogant and disrespectful when doing that so that the devil will not introduce his leaven.

This is never about gender disparity but about God's authority. God is so much concerned about female folks as well. Here is what His Word said.

1 Peter 3:7 "Likewise, ye husbands, dwell with them according to knowledge, giving honour unto the wife, as unto the weaker vessel, and as being heirs together of the grace of life; that your prayers be not hindered."

God is an Administrator. He is concerned with how the home will be governed. He is not the author of confusion. This is why all the conference chatters by gender activists have failed to yield expected results. God's concept can never be set aside for any reason whatsoever.

The Apostle Paul in his general epistle to the Ephesians said:

Ephesians 5:23-24 "For the husband is the head of the wife, even as Christ is the head of the church: and he is the saviour of the body. Therefore as the church is subject unto Christ, so let the wives be to their own husbands in everything."

We can also learn from what the Apostle Peter said in his first general epistle.

1 Peter 5:24 "Therefore as the church is subject unto Christ, so let the wives be to their own husbands in everything."

1 Peter 3:5 "For after this manner in the old time the holy women also, who trusted in God, adorned themselves, being in subjection unto their own husbands. Even as Sara obeyed Abraham, calling him lord: whose daughters ye are, as long as ye do well, and are not afraid with any amazement".

So don't treat people any way you want. This can engender strife and even lead to malicious behavior. Verse eight below seemed to summarize all that is required never to be disrespectful to anyone.

1 Peter 3:8 "Finally, be ye all of one mind, having compassion one for another, love as brethren, be pitiful, be courteous: Not rendering evil for evil, or railing for railing: but contrariwise blessing; knowing that ye are thereunto called, that ye should inherit a blessing".

No one likes to be disrespected no matter the age or gender.

Nagging

Nagging can be a very strong indicator of an internal crisis. It announces the presence of malice and other behavioral vices. It is like a wine bottle shaken with the cork on. The person involved always has something to complain about. Feeling like nobody really does what he or she wants. Always in "compare and contrast" mode. They are not usually happy. The devil's yeast breeds well in this environment. Love is manifested with difficulty. Life becomes unbearable for both parties.

The Scripture paints a vivid picture of this scenario in:

Proverbs 21:9 "It is better to dwell in a corner of the housetop, than with a brawling woman in a wide house."

Proverbs 21:19 "It is better to dwell in the wilderness, than with a contentious and an angry woman."

Proverbs 27:15 "A continual dripping in a very rainy day and a contentious woman are alike."

It is not only women who are contentious. Men and even children are affected alike.

People have abandoned their houses and even committed suicide because of nagging partners. Some will start nursing malicious thoughts like wishing evil on himself or his wife.

Here is the truth; the irrational decision is imminent whenever you drive your spouse into a marital desert place, or in fleeing for peace sake. Escape into a corner of the rooftop.

Other malice triggers to watch include spousal insincerity, undue comparisons, suspicious tendencies, wrong attitude to money, infidelity, secrecy amongst other things.

The remedy to this hydra-headed monster is not far-fetched.

The Scriptures below proffer lasting solutions for any kind of malice. They are both preventive and curative if obeyed. God is the best marriage counselor ever known. Here is His counsel on malice.

1 Corinthians 14:20 "Brethren, be not children in understanding: howbeit in malice be ye children, but in understanding be men."

Ephesians 4:31-32 "Let all bitterness, and wrath, and anger, and clamour, and evil speaking, be put away from you, with all malice: And be ye kind one to another, tenderhearted, forgiving one another, even as God for Christ's sake hath forgiven you."

Ephesians 4:26 -27 "Be ye angry and sin not: let not sun go down on your wrath. Neither give place to the devil."

Titus 3:3 "For we ourselves also were sometimes

foolish, disobedient, deceived, serving divers lusts and pleasures, living in malice and envy, hateful, and hating one another." Titus 3:3 shows that change is possible, irrespective of your current lifestyle.

1 Peter 2:1 "Wherefore laying aside all malice, and all guile, and hypocrisies, and envies, all evil speaking."

Colossians 3:8 "But now ye also put off all these; anger, wrath, malice, blasphemy, filthy communication out of your mouth."

Brethren, the Word of God is powerful. It is sharper than a two-edged sword.

So join me in making these solemn declarations over your family in Jesus Name.

SOLEMN DECLARATIONS

1. Today I stand in my priestly office as a servant of the most high God to cancel and nullify every satanic manipulation over your family.
2. Let all bitterness, and wrath, and anger, and clamour, nagging and evil speaking, be put away from you from now in the Mighty Name of Jesus.
3. The noise of joy that used to be heard in your homes shall again be restored in the name of Jesus.

Peace be onto your house Amen!

CHAPTER 5

THE FAMILY ALTAR. WHOSE RESPONSIBILITY?

The altar refers to a place of meeting between mortals and a chosen deity. These days, such meeting places are commonly found at road junctions, under the trees, on mountain tops, on rocks and so on. Some other worshipers have their altars right in their houses.

Altars can be personally or jointly owned. Most large or mega-altars usually have a priest attending. The priests function as middlemen between the gods and the worshipers. They become consulting oracles who know and speak the mind of the gods.

Different altars may represent different deities. In **Acts 17**, Paul describes how the Athenians, wanting to make sure they hadn't missed a god and no deity was left out, constructed an altar to an unknown god.

Acts 17:22-23 "Then Paul stood in the midst of Mars' hill, and said, Ye men of Athens, I perceive that in all things ye are too superstitious. For as I passed by, and beheld your devotions, I found an altar with this inscription, TO THE UNKNOWN GOD. Whom, therefore, ye ignorantly worship, him declare I unto you."

The Nature And Purpose Of A Home Altar

Contrary to what was practiced in Athens, a home altar is not necessarily a consecrated piece of furniture mounted in a corner of a house with holy inscriptions. Rather, it is a place of fellowship with the one, true God of the Bible.

The Man As A Non-Seminarian Priest

Within the home and family, the husband functions as the priest. He is to take charge and perform the functions of a priest. This is how every head of the family should see himself.

You don't need a title to assume that office. You are God's lesson Teacher at home. God arranged it this way in order to preserve for Himself a generation that will fear Him and worship Him as the only true God.

Look at what the Psalmist said in **Psalm 78:6-7** "That the generation to come might know them, even the children which should be born; who should arise and declare them to their children: That they might set their hope in God, and not forget the works of God, but keep his commandments."

This is the essence of the family altar.

In **Deuteronomy 11:2** God told the Israelites clearly that it was their responsibility to pass on His knowledge to the unborn generations. They should serve as Jehovah's witness.

"And know ye this day: for I speak not with your children which have not known, and which have not seen the chastisement of the LORD your God, His greatness, His mighty hand, and His stretched out arm…"

God made them realize that the unborn children needed to be told all that happened in Egypt. How He divided the Red Sea with His Mighty hands and caused Pharaoh's choicest chariots and their riders to sink like lead in the waters.

His mighty deeds. The signs and the wonders must be given an overwhelming publicity.

Deuteronomy. 11:18-19 highlighted what should be done in order to achieve that. He said to them

"Therefore shall ye lay up these my words in your heart and in your soul, and bind them for a sign upon your hand, that they may be as frontlets between your eyes. And ye shall teach them your children, speaking of them when thou sittest in thine house, and when thou walkest by the way, when thou liest down, and when thou risest up."

What a beautiful home picture. But in order to occupy this Honorable position, the man must know and be known by God too.

God spoke about such man in **Genesis 18:19** "For I know him, that he will command his children and his household after him, and they shall keep the way of the LORD, to do justice and judgment; that the LORD may bring upon Abraham that which he hath spoken of him". I call it "the Genesis 18 & 19 mandate."

When God said "I know him" talking about Abraham, it means Abraham could be relied upon to execute the above mandate. This is the position every man should earnestly desire to occupy in the mind of God. The wife should help the man to realize these, and in his absence take up the responsibility as the deputy.

Delegated Authority

The authority to represent God is given to man by God Himself. This is the order by which God extends His influence and control to every home unit on earth. God is worried when the man abdicates this responsibility for anything less.

Paul the Apostle has this to say.

Ephesians 5:23 "For the husband is the head of the wife, even as Christ is the head of the church: and he is the saviour of the body."

The above position is not contestable. Our beloved wives should settle this in their hearts. Their support is required as this is God-ordained. God is not the author of confusion. Therefore, any man-made declaration, summit, or chatter that negates the above chapter should not be given expression in godly homes. God's purpose was clear. He sent a helpmeet not a helpmate.

Genesis 2:18 "And the LORD God said, It is not good that the man should be alone; I will make him an helpmeet for him."

Wives allow your husbands to be the priest and you will get more than the offal. This is just natural. In most African countries, it is a taboo to be a queen without a king. So facilitate the coronation of your husband and "Her Royal Highness" will become your next title. God is not complaining about you being the deputy priest in the house.

Some women are more spiritual than their husbands. Excellent! But that should be harnessed for a quality and robust fellowship at the altar. They should operate under delegated authority. The husband should be encouraged to take up his responsibility.

Dan Benson, in his book "*The Total Man,*" quoted a Spanish proverb thus: "Woe to the house where the hen crows and the rooster keeps still." This sounds abnormal and unnatural doesn't it? So the rooster should wake up and occupy his priestly office and begin to crow. He should take charge and direct the affairs of his family according to God-given mandates.

The Eden Crisis

The Garden of Eden was the abode of the first family on earth. They lived in peace and harmony. Everything was going well for them. It was a mini paradise.

Adam was in charge. He was both the priest and the garden administrator. He was alone in this service before God thought of sending him a helper.

Genesis 2:15 "And the LORD God took the man, and put him into the garden of Eden to dress it and to keep it."

He was also to come up with a system by which the animals would be named. God gave him a free hand and adopted his nomenclature.

Genesis 2:19 "And out of the ground the LORD God formed every beast of the field and every fowl of the air, and brought them unto Adam to see what he would call them: and whatsoever Adam called every living creature, that was the name thereof."

God has no problem with anybody becoming great as long as such greatness is expressed in absolute loyalty to His instructions. We find one of those loyalty tests in the following scriptures.

Genesis 2:16-17 "And the LORD God commanded the man, saying, Of every tree of the garden thou mayest freely eat: But of the tree of the knowledge of good and evil, thou shalt not eat of it: for in the day that thou eatest thereof thou shalt surely die."

"And the Lord God commanded the man..."

God does not throw His instructions into the air. He is a perfect example of an excellent administrator. Someone would have to be held responsible for the success or failure of the garden. The same is applicable in any family setting. God wants to hold somebody responsible. And that is the man.

When the serpent visited the garden, he made the woman sign a deal behind the husband who is the Chief Executive Officer. He made her fail the only integrity test the family has upheld for a very long time.

In most organizations, certain major decisions are never taken in isolation. The CEO must be involved. The organization's core belief systems should not be thrown overboard because a visitor challenged its authenticity. God said if you eat "…ye shall die," but the serpent said, "…ye shall not surely die." I feel like asking for the whereabouts of the first priest and the CEO of this garden. Something that will plunge future unborn generations into eternal regrets was about to happen. Hmmm! I thought I would hear the mother of all mankind say, "Excuse me Mr. Serpent, I will discuss this with my husband and will you come back when he returns?"

Genesis 3:4-5 "And the serpent said unto the woman, Ye shall not surely die: For God doth know that in the day ye eat thereof, then your eyes shall be opened, and ye shall be as gods, knowing good and evil."

That was an outright Indictment of God. But the Serpent had a plan. He wanted to destroy them by making them set aside God's instructions in disobedience. And the serpent did succeed.

Porous Homes Are Vulnerable

The Christian home is, of course, more than just a blessed shelter and a refuge against evil. It is a sanctuary amidst a godless and Christless world, where the precious souls of children are kept and preserved from the daily bombardment of evil and defiling influences from the society.

Unfortunately, many fathers and mothers are preoccupied with business and material things that they take little or no time for reading or meditating on the scriptures for their own spiritual needs and those of their children. This leaves the home porous and vulnerable to all manners of attacks.

Genesis 3:8 "And they heard the voice of the LORD God walking in the garden in the cool of the day: and Adam and his wife hid themselves from the presence of the LORD God amongst the trees of the garden."

In **Genesis 3:9** "The LORD God called unto Adam, and said unto him, Where art thou?"

The same question goes to all head of families today. God is asking ,"You, Mr. Adam, Where art thou?" We are all free to put our names in the place of Adam and answer the question sincerely.

It was like God was asking Adam, "Where art thou?" you were not seen at the morning oblation?

My father in the Lord, Dr. John Akpami once told a story of what happened in his own house. He abandoned the family altar to his wife and concentrated on what he termed were more spiritual activities. These activities include prolonged prayers with speaking in tongues, personal Bible study and so on.

He was shocked to hear one of the children telling his wife that their Daddy is the pastor in the church while Mummy is their pastor at home. It was at this point, according to him, the implications of his actions dawned on him. He resolved from that day to resume his pastoral responsibility at home.

Where were you:
- when your children became wayward?
- when the serpent came in subtly and thwarted the instructions you were given?
- when my orders and instructions were set aside in thy house and worldliness became the order of the day?

She Gave Me Of The Tree, And I Did Eat

Genesis 3:10 "And he said, I heard thy voice in the garden, and I was afraid, because I was naked; and I hid myself."

Hiding from God is never the solution. Blaming our spouses is not either. What God wants is a sincere repentance and a deep commitment to the upbringing of your family according to the God-given mandate.

Don't you ever forget that the genuineness of your love for your spouse is measured by the level of loyalty God gets as a result.

Gen.3:12 "And the man said, The woman whom thou gavest to be with me, she gave me of the tree, and I did eat."

This excuse is not love. Love should not be blind to the instructions of God.

What Apostle Paul said in **Ephesians 4:13** is applicable here.

Ephesians 4:13 "Till we all come in the unity of the faith, and of the knowledge of the Son of God, unto a perfect man, unto the measure of the stature of the fulness of Christ:

14 That we henceforth be no more children, tossed to and fro, and carried about with every wind of doctrine, by the sleight of men, and cunning craftiness, whereby they lie in wait to deceive;

15 But speaking the truth in love, may grow up into him in all things, which is the head, even Christ."

My counsel to the man, the home priest, the God-appointed CEO, is found in the scripture above.

Till we all come (now your family)... unto the measure of the stature of the fullness of Christ; don't give up your role as the chief home builder. The Lord will reward you for it.

A Moment Of Prayer

We can make these declarations together:

1. Lord, thank you for my family, of which I am the head.
2. Lord, I am sorry for my nonchalant attitude. Please, forgive my inability to function in my office as the head of the family.
3. In the name of Jesus, I rise up with this knowledge to reclaim my family from the hand of the enemy.
4. Lord, I make this solemn declaration today "...but as for me and my house, we will serve the LORD. (**Joshua 24:15**)

CHAPTER 6

DEBT IS A BURDEN NOT MEANT FOR YOUR FAMILY

Debt burden is one burden that doesn't attract the sympathy of many volunteers. Helping hands are not readily available in spite of numerous biblical commandments. In most cases, the bearer is left alone, groaning under such burdens.

Instead of **Galatians 6:2** which says:

"Bear ye one another's burdens, and so fulfill the law of Christ,"the verse of the day becomes **Galatians 6:5,** "For every man shall bear his own burden."

Beloved, you will be making a very big mistake if you borrow money or incur debts with your eyes on the church tithes and offerings. I don't know of any church congregation that raises money for debt cancellation. What is usual is preaching and praying for debts to be canceled. So don't allow debt to drag your family into the cold.

When Interest Rate Becomes a Burden Rate

Some debts come with an additional burden. This occurs when interest is accruable. The burden increases in a direct proportion to the interest. The interest rate becomes the burden rate. Friends, no investment deal survives high-interest rates.

A web publication on 28th November, 2012, defined **debt burden** as "The cost of interest payment on debt." ***www.economicshelp.org***

Some folks have no problem with borrowing. I have a friend who boasted of his plans to borrow money from people. He had the right message and the right approach. But he lacked the ability to repay the money owed. He told people he was not ashamed of borrowing. He said what is more important is to repay the money owed. It wasn't long before this same brother owed everybody in the neighborhood.

The result was a public disgrace, family embarrassment and reproach to the body of Christ. Men have hidden under the bed on hearing the voice of their creditors. Some fled the city, relocating to strange and unfamiliar territories. Others have committed suicide. What can be more humiliating than that? Child of God, this is not the will of God for you. Here is His covenant plan for you.

Deuteronomy 15:6 "For the LORD thy God blesseth thee, as he promised thee: and thou shalt lend unto many nations, but thou shalt not borrow, and thou shalt reign over many nations, but they shall not reign over thee."

Obey These Principles if You Want to Live A Debt-Free Life

Make sure you operate within the covenant principles.

The moment you give your life to Jesus, you become God's responsibility by the covenant which was ratified by His blood. The blood of Jesus. Remember how you became responsible for that little baby of yours right from the day your wife gave birth to the child? You didn't do that when your neighbor's wife delivered her baby. Why? Because you were not directly responsible. He was not your child. Someone else takes charge. Probably, his covenant father.

God is your covenant father. Here is what he said:

Jeremiah 29:11 "For I know the thoughts that I think toward you, saith the LORD, thoughts of peace, and not of evil, to give you an expected end."

That is the Father's mindset. Therefore the sonship mentality is required in order to receive the Father's Blessing. This covenant relationship gives you open access to the world of riches of the Father.

The kingdom wealth bestowed upon a kingdom child comes from God the King and Father. Here is what the King has to say.

Deuteronomy 8:18 "But thou shalt remember the LORD thy God: for it is he that giveth thee power to get wealth, that he may establish his covenant which he sware unto thy fathers, as it is this day.

Friends, 'remember' means bringing again into consciousness. God gives you the covenant power to get *wealth* NOT *debt.* You must always remember this. It calls for absolute dependency. But when you work outside the covenant provisions, you get debt instead of wealth.

God's servant, Bishop David Oyedepo in his book **'Breaking Financial Hardship'** clarifies this point. He says "Covenant wealth is not an issue of luck or chance. It has no bearing on the country you are living in. The economic policy of the nation has no relevance to it. It has to do with your willingness and obedience to the terms of that Godly covenant."

This is the Kingdom's operational guidelines for a life of abundance and financial sustainability.

Wrong Decisions

My father in the Lord Dr. John Akpami, in one of his messages, said: "Life is not in the great messages we have listened to, but in the great decisions we make after such great messages." This is why people attend great meetings and still cannot meet with God.

Success or failure is a product of the decisions we have taken at certain times in our lives. The small things we do on daily bases are summed up for us and brought forward. The total is what we ultimately become. So watch your financial behavior.

Inability to Plan Ahead (Budgeting)

According to an adage in the southern part of

Nigeria; "Money said he likes to be in the hands of the fools, so that he can spend them, instead of the fools spending him."

Friends, you are the one to spend the money; but where there is no planning, the reverse becomes the case. Money begins to spend you, putting pressure on the lives of the people around you.

The Lord Jesus Christ illustrated this perfectly in the story below.

Building a Tower Rather than Buying a Tower.

Luke 14:28-30 "For which of you, intending to build a TOWER, sitteth not down first, and counteth the cost, whether he have sufficient to finish it?

29 Lest haply, after he hath laid the foundation, and is not able to finish it, all that behold it begin to mock him,

30 Saying, 'This man began to build, and was not able to finish.'"

What a wonderful illustration made by our Lord. To some people, planning means making a long list of what you want to buy before entering the grocery store. Are you sure you know what the Lord was talking about? Building a tower is different from buying a tower. These are two different things.

The man who wants to buy a tower will concentrate on two things. The design and the amount. He stops at the facility, and straightaway calls the facility manager for the price.

75

Whereas, the tower builder will first sit down, analyze his concept and then determine the cost of construction. Bringing in different experts at different levels and stages. Why? Of course, he wouldn't want to be financially strapped and be forced to abandon the project. Or resort to borrowing at high rates if he must continue.

Spending Habits

Financial Experts will not need an oracle to predict your imminent financial crisis. All they need to do is to watch your spending habits. You will end up in debt if you are the type that spends money as it comes in. Such people are only concerned about what they spend instead of what they earn. And because your spending drives your earnings; you are obligated to source out extra funds in order to meet your obligations. Those extra funds are what you call debt.

Riotous Living (Financial Recklessness)

Many people live as if there is no tomorrow.
Here is what the Lord said in **Luke 15:11-14:**
"And he said, A certain man had two sons: And the younger of them said to his father, Father, give me the portion of goods that falleth to me. And he divided unto them his living. And not many days after the younger son gathered all together, and took his journey into a far country, and there wasted his substance with

riotous living. And when he had spent all, there arose a mighty famine in that land; and he began to be in want."

The Lord said, "and when he had spent all, there arose a mighty famine in that land; and he began to be in want."

This is the point at which debt occurs.

Nobody in his right mind will like to eat with the pigs. Your money can run out and yet there is no famine in the land. Friends can afford to lend you some money. You wouldn't need the pigs. But when you have spent all, and there arises a mighty famine... my brother you need the pigs to survive.

I pray this will not be your portion, in Jesus Name.

We just have to be cautious. I know many people who were very wealthy in years past, who are now eating with the pigs. When I ask to know why the downturn, the only answer I get is 'financial recklessness'.

You know some of these people in your community.

They have this common mentality: "Instead of it being in the bank, let it be in the belly."

1 Corinthians 6:13 "Meat for the belly, and the belly for meats: but God shall destroy both it and them..."

Greed

The Bible did not spare the greedy. Greedy men don't treasure small profit ventures. They want to hit it big. And if the business fails, everyone goes down. They bring needless pain and untold hardship to their entire household. A greedy man is always gathering both the things he needs and those he doesn't need.

I once saw a picture of a hunter who was coming home with an elephant on his head and was struggling to catch a grasshopper with his legs. Greed is still different from living in a fine manner. Consider this scripture below:

Isaiah 55:2 "Why pay money for something that will not nourish you? Why spend your hard-earned money on something that will not satisfy? Listen carefully to me and eat what is nourishing! Enjoy fine food!" (NET)

Proverbs 15:27 "He that is greedy of gain troubleth his own house; but he that hateth gifts shall live."

Yes, we are the ones troubling our own houses because of our greedy decisions.

God is not against those who make a profit, but He is against those greedy of gain.

Pursuing Unrealistic Dreams

Unrealistic dreams and goals are never realized. Resources are washed down the drain for another trial. Their dreams are usually outside the will of God for their lives. They set unattainable goals in frustration. Some call it faith. But, if it is faith, it will work because faith originates from God.

Wanting to be Like Someone Else

2 Corinthians 10:12 "For we dare not make ourselves of the number, or compare ourselves with some that commend themselves: but they measuring themselves by themselves, and comparing themselves among themselves, are not wise."

High-mindedness

Friends, I have observed that everything God is against, will always be against us if we neglect it. Some people believe that high-mindedness means thinking big like God. They say "God is a big God and if it is not big then it is not God." My brother, this is a devilish philosophy.

The Apostle Paul said to Timothy in **1 Timothy 6:5** "Perverse disputings of men of corrupt minds, and destitute of the truth, supposing that gain is godliness: from such withdraw thyself."

Of course, God is not only big but mighty. He owns the heavens and earth but, you have just a rented three bedroom flat. He is the owner of the cattle on a thousand hills; but, the last meat you ate was a few kilos from a grocery shop. He is the owner of silver and gold, including the ones in your pocket. He said if He needs money or food He will not consult you. Come on brother! You need to wake up and embrace the gospel truth that high-mindedness is a sin.

I know a friend who will do everything to duplicate

everything he sees in your house in his own house. He will start depositing money in installments with the dealers in order to have the same thing as you have.

The good news is that the great God I described above is your Father. That position does not make you a prodigal son but a principled son.

High-mindedness is what you have whenever a desire is sponsored by greed instead of faith. Beware, this has landed many in debt.

Lack of Contentment

1 Timothy 6:6-11 "But godliness with contentment is great gain. For we brought nothing into this world, and it is certain we can carry nothing out. And having food and raiment let us be therewith content. But they that will be rich fall into temptation and a snare, and into many foolish and hurtful lusts, which drown men in destruction and perdition. For the love of money is the root of all evil: which while some coveted after, they have erred from the faith, and pierced themselves through with many sorrows. But thou, O man of God, flee these things; and follow after righteousness, godliness, faith, love, patience, meekness."

The gains of godliness with contentment is unquantifiable. They will save you from erring from the faith, and piercing yourselves through with many sorrows. The body of Christ should receive the above scripture as a guide to harmonious and peaceful living.

"And having food and raiment let us be therewith content" I call this "The normal minimum affluence level."

Yes, for "food and raiment" be happy. If you are not walking naked in the street, be happy; if you have eaten today, be happy. This is because you are far ahead of millions of people who may go to bed tonight without food.

Saint Luke's Gospel says **Luke 12:15** "And he said unto them, Take heed, and beware of covetousness: for a man's life consisteth not in the abundance of the things which he possesseth."

Free Loans (yielding to the tantalizing offer of financial institutions)

Banks and other financial institutions are fond of luring people into obtaining loans that usually become debt traps. Debt is the prize of every 'free loan,' so do everything to avoid it. The implications are huge.

The widow, wife of the late prophet, had a very sour story to tell.

2 Kings 4:1-7 "Now there cried a certain woman of the wives of the sons of the prophets unto Elisha, saying, Thy servant my husband is dead, and thou knowest that thy servant did fear the LORD: and the creditor is come to take unto him my two sons to be bondsmen."

Beloved, what can be worse than the above situation? That she is a widow is enough affliction.

Left with two sons to care for, including herself. If this man happened to be a Pastor in our days, it seemed as if the congregation abandoned her to fate. No one was willing to help her out.

In case, you are wondering about the integrity of the prophet; hear his testimony. "Thy servant, my husband, is dead, and thou knowest that thy servant did fear the LORD" No questionable character. A prophet with integrity. And Elisha knew it.

Friends, debt is a subtle agent of slavery. The scripture below is a strong warning to all and sundry. Heed to it and save your soul and family from impending lamentations.

Proverbs 22:7 "The rich ruleth over the poor, and the borrower is servant to the lender."

Did I hear you say, "God forbid?" Of course He would like to, but you are the *first* one to forbid it.

Undue Status and Class Consciousness

A jobless graduate who goes to eat in a five-star hotel just because he is a graduate will soon go to jail. Unfortunately, most couples run their homes that way bringing all manners of insults upon themselves. Most financial adjustments are driven by prevailing circumstances. Borrowing becomes inevitable when driven by class and status.

Jumping into a Business Without Proper Assessment and Training

In business, you must learn in order to earn. Every business has its own module. And that has to be studied. You will need counsel from those who have done similar businesses before.

I will never forget my experience in the poultry business some years back. A brother who claimed to be a poultry expert, convinced my church into starting such a business. He was only telling us how lucrative the business was. For him, there was no failure rate. In fact, if there was any rate, it could not be more than 0%-1%.

This opportunity came at a time when I was doing everything to financially empower the church and its members. We didn't waste time to plunge into the business as a church. Members were asked to buy shares and they did so. The young man told us that in 4-6 weeks' time, we would all be smiling on the way to the bank.

Well, to cut a long story short, we lost all the birds. Our 'expert' disappeared until a later date. We later found out that he never had any reliable training in the poultry business. Those of us who loaned money for this investment ended up in debt.

Gambling

When you use your traveling money for a casino; trekking home should not be considered a punishment. God is not a gambler. In His kingdom, things happen by His choice, not by chance. His children are not just lucky. They are blessed deliberately by the Almighty.

Turning Your Back On God

The prophet's wife must have given up all hope by now. Some of us would have turned our back on God. We would have cursed the church and the leadership. She could have rained abuses at all her husband's course mates in the School of Prophecy, where her husband ones was a student. But this woman was different. Here is what the Bible said about her.

2 Kings 4:1-7 "Now there cried a certain woman of the wives of the sons of the prophets unto Elisha..." I wished she had done this early enough before the death of her husband. Who knows if the life of the husband would have been spared; as some people would say that his demise was due to the heavy debt burden. It is possible they were busy figuring out possible ways out of the debt situation.

We are not told what dragged the family into that nasty financial mess. If it happened in our day, the obvious reasons might include the payment of school fees, health issues, or some pressing domestic needs. The widow cried to God through His prophet for help. Friends, every physical problem has a spiritual undertone. There is no situation on this planet that does not respond to prayer.

If you are reading this book now, there is still hope for you. You will not die in debt. The banks will not come after your properties. Cry to God. What you need may just be an instruction.

2 Kings 4:2-7 "And Elisha said unto her, What shall I do for thee? Tell me, what hast thou in the house? And she said, Thine handmaid hath not anything in the house, save a pot of oil.

3 He said, Go, borrow thee vessels abroad of all thy neighbours, even empty vessels; borrow not a few.

4 And when thou art come in, thou shalt shut the door upon thee and upon thy sons, and shalt pour out into all those vessels, and thou shalt set aside that which is full.

5 So she went from him, and shut the door upon her and upon her sons, who brought the vessels to her; and she poured out.

6 And it came to pass, when the vessels were full, that she said unto her son, Bring me yet a vessel. And he said unto her; There is not a vessel more. And the oil stayed."

The Elshaddai, the all-breasted one, and the all-sufficient God showed up with an overwhelming mysterious display of the supernatural. Brethren, as you can see, most financial miracles happen behind closed doors. Your case will not be different. The God of the widow and Elisha is not dead.

Sell The Oil And Pay Thy Debt

2 Kings 4:7 "Then she came and told the man of God. And he said, Go, sell the oil, and pay thy debt, and live thou and thy children of the rest."

Every miracle from above has a purpose to fulfill here below. Miracles are sent to remove obstacles. The instruction was clear. "Sell the oil and pay thy debt."

Your oil may be different. It may be one of those cars, landed properties, or even personal clothes that might do the magic. It could be one of your expensive cell phones. The truth is that God may have sent those properties ahead of the evil day to serve as a bailout. There is always room for replacement as soon as the situation improves.

Don't misappropriate the miracle, The instruction still remains. "Sell the oil and pay thy debt." It is never, sell the oil and buy new shoes. Don't also sell your oil on credit at such times otherwise: the creditors will come after your children.

Illustrative Meaning of DEBT

D...Devil's

Every debt has a devil in it, if is not properly managed. Not everyone can stand the constant harassment of creditors. The devil will tell you there is nothing to worry about. Get the services or the goods and pay at the end of the month. But the salary was delayed that month, and you ran into trouble with people. The devil didn't tell you that will happen, did he? You know he wouldn't.

E...Estimates

The devil is a bad mathematician. Don't make him your quantity surveyor. He does not use righteous indices in his computations. You will definitely run at a loss. And he laughs at you. But if you use the Holy Spirit, you will always be smiling.

B...Brought

The devil is good at bringing up businesses that will run people down. He will paint a very lucrative picture, and tell you that it is worth selling all that you have. And before you know it you are finished. He wants every child of God to suffer perpetually.

T...Tarnish

The objective is to TARNISH your image. Yes! To tarnish your image. He wants to make you believe that God no longer cares for you. But God's position is different according to Apostle Paul as seen below:

Phil. 4:19 "But my God shall supply all your need according to his riches in glory by Christ Jesus."

Borrowing As A Bailout

People tend to postpone certain financial harassment by borrowing to pay off existing debt. It gives a false sense of relief. Borrowing is a direct way of incurring debt. The purpose may look reasonable, positive and laudable as we saw in the Gilgal School of Prophesy. The student prophets wanted to expand their hostel. Didn't they? Just like you would want to borrow money and expand your business. But the moment you did that, exchange rates changed. A ban is placed on imported or exported goods. In fact, your axe head fell into the river. What is left for you at this point is to borrow more money from one source to repay the first lender. May God save you if the Bank of Heaven did not intervene.

2 Kings 6:5 "But as one was felling a beam, the axe head fell into the water: and he cried, and said, Alas, master! for it was borrowed."

I can't imagine what would have happened if there was no Elisha in that operation. The entire expansion program would have been truncated, leaving a debt burden behind.

May I pray for you dearly beloved?

1   Every plan of hell to plunge you and your family into debt, be stopped in Jesus' Mighty Name, Amen!

2. For those of you who are already trapped, I command the debt trap to be shattered in Jesus' Name, Amen!

3. May the Almighty God multiply the oil in your hand. You will sell them, and you will pay your debt, in Jesus' Name, Amen!

4. The creditor will not harass you. They will not come after your properties. None of your family members will be used to settle the debt in Jesus' Name, Amen!

Friends, don't forget "debt is not a burden meant for your family."

CHAPTER 7

MR. AND MRS. ANANIAS

Sure, this does not sound like any family name that you know. I have not come across any family name like that either. The names are not common in my locale. However, in practice, we tend to have more Sapphiras married to Ananias's now than in the Bible days. Most couples today behave more like Mr. and Mrs. Ananias.

Acts 5:1-11 "But a certain man named Ananias, with Sapphira his wife, sold a possession,

2 And kept back part of the price, his wife also being privy to it, and brought a certain part, and laid it at the apostles' feet.

3 but Peter said, Ananias, why hath Satan filled thine heart to lie to the Holy Ghost, and to keep back part of the price of the land?

4 Whiles it remained, was it not thine own? And

after it was sold, was it not in thine own power? Thou hast not lied unto men, but God.

5 And Ananias hearing these words fell down, and gave up the ghost: and great fear came on all them that heard these things.

6 And the young men arose, wound him up, and carried him out, and buried him."

They buried him according to their custom, a description of which is found in **John 19:40:** "Then took they the body of Jesus, and wound it in linen clothes with the spices, as the manner of the Jews is to bury."

7 And it was about the space of three hours after, when his wife, came in.

8 And Peter answered unto her, Tell me whether ye sold the land for so much? And she said, Yea, for so much.

9 Then Peter said unto her, how is it that ye have agreed together to tempt the Spirit of the Lord? Behold, the feet of them which have buried thy husband are at the door, and shall carry thee out.

10 Then fell she down straightway at his feet, and yielded up the ghost: and the young men came in, and found her dead, and, carrying her forth, buried her beside her husband.

11 And great fear came upon all the church, and upon as many, as heard these things."

The Tragic Service That Was Forgotten Too Soon

That very day the Holy Spirit delivered a teaching on 'The Fear Of God' with a very tragic illustration. The lives of Mr. and Mrs. Ananias were used to drive home the lessons.

Hmmm! You are cold like me, aren't you? But, who can battle with the Lord? Who can question His actions? Our beloved brother Job seemed to throw more light on what our safe position should be.

He said in **Job 9:12** "Behold, he taketh away, who can hinder him? Who will say unto him, What doest thou?"

Unfortunately, some couples have yet to learn this age-old lesson. Where is the fear of God today? Men and brethren, we don't need a repeat of such a tragic lecture to change our callous attitude and behavior towards our God. If not for the mercies of our God, most church meetings would end up with sudden funeral services. Thank God the Holy Spirit did not make that a pattern.

The Psalmist said in **Psalm 130:3** "If thou, LORD, shouldest mark iniquities, O Lord, who shall stand?"

We all know this fact. Adjournment of a trial does not mean acquittal. That our case has been adjourned does not mean we are acquitted. Forgiveness should have been a panacea if we had harkened to the instruction "Go home and sin no more"

Back to the unfortunate incident. Imagine yourself attending the same fellowship with the late couple.

You were even there the day everyone was given the opportunity to pledge what they were going to give to the Lord. You can still vividly remember how Ananias stood up that day, and rocked the entire congregation with soul piercing and heavenly bound "P...r...a...i...s...e the Lord." The brethren responded, and their hallelujah followed the same frequency. The description above is a common scenario in most African churches, where 'Amen' and 'Hallelujah' are celebrated.

In the end, Ananias made his pledge. He pledged to sell his property and bring the money for the work of the apostles. God has no problem with that. But listening to Apostle Peter's interrogation, you will observe that the Spirit of God was not particular about how much they brought before Peter, but about for how much the property was sold.

"And Peter answered unto her, Tell me whether ye sold the land for so much? And she said, Yea, for so much."

What is the Apostle Peter up to? Some of you may question, Why is he getting personal with Ananias family? He was not a Real Estate Agent. All Peter needed to do was receive the money and let the work of the Lord move on.

Friends, before you crucify Peter, we need to understand that this was first the move of the Holy Spirit. There was no other way to describe what was going on at that time.

Look at this:

Acts 4:33-37 "With great power, the apostles gave witness of the resurrection of the Lord Jesus: and great grace was upon them all.

34 Neither was there any among them that lacked: for as many as were possessors of lands or houses sold them and brought the prices of the things that were sold,

35 And laid them down at the apostles' feet: and distribution was made unto every man according as he had need.

36 And Joses, who by the apostles was surnamed Barnabas, (which is, being interpreted, "the son of consolation"), a Levite, and of the country of Cyprus,

37 Having land, sold it, and brought the money, and laid it at the apostles' feet."

Brethren, this was not about Apostle Peter, but the Surveyor General of the whole wide world talking through him. He was the real Person in charge of the deal. He also brought the buyers with great offers. Because He wants to take care of His church. The issue is in keeping back some.

Brethren, we often fall into a similar trap. Some will pledge to sell their belongings in order to support the work of God. But to their amazement; the Holy Spirit will bring a crazy buyer who would pay an amount far much higher than the value of the goods.

Let's say the lot fell on one of your oldest cars. In your heart, even a blind man, cannot pay five thousand dollars for the car, ($5,000) but now someone is paying twenty thousand dollars ($20,000) with excitement. You can see that this is unusual. So if you have pledged to sell and bring the price, then get ready to remit the twenty thousand dollars ($20,000) to the Lord.

God is not a careless listener. When you stand to make your promises, vows or pledges, God keeps His ears wide open to hear what you have to say. His eyes also beam directly into your heart to know if there are other non-verbalized Terms and Conditions.

This is why He warned in **Deuteronomy 23:21-23**: "When thou shalt vow a vow unto the LORD thy God, thou shalt not slack to pay it: for the LORD thy God will surely require it of thee, and it would be sin in thee. But if thou shalt forbear to vow, it shall be no sin in thee. That which is gone out of thy lips thou shalt keep and perform; even a freewill offering, according as thou hast vowed unto the LORD thy God, which thou hast promised with thy mouth."

On the other hand, if your pledge is to sell and, out of the proceeds, bring an offering, then you will not be accused. But that does not mean you should lie about the price at which it was sold when that selling price is requested of you.

"...for as many as were possessors of lands or houses sold them, and brought the prices of the things that were sold..."

Others brought the *prices* of the things that were sold, but Ananias presented a falsified figure. He kept back some.

The Spirit of God wants us to be righteous even in our giving. He hates deceit and falsehood.

Peter asked, "Ananias... why has satan filled your heart?" Meaning, for behind every lie there is the working of satan. This is the truth we must tell ourselves.

So, husbands and wives save yourselves. You are joined in a holy wedlock. You are not partners in wickedness. For why should Mrs. Ananias also die in that meeting? Why did God kill her?

Mrs. Ananias was sentenced because she connived with her husband Mr. Ananias to lie to the Holy Spirit. As far as heaven is concerned, she was not qualified to live any longer. She was to bell the cat, but she failed. She became an accomplice, aiding and abetting the crime. She joined herself in the suit against the Holy Spirit. Little did they know that Peter was just a figurehead. In fact, a messenger The Holy Spirit was the actual person in charge. So those who unite with their spouses in their sins should not expect a separation when judgment comes.

Proverbs 11:21 "Though hand join in hand, the wicked will not go unpunished..."

She failed heaven in her mission to Ananias as a helpmeet, and she expired. Ananias carried her along in the transaction. But she didn't or couldn't stop the evil deal. If she was around in the fellowship at the time her husband testified, maybe she could have said something different. But the Spirit of God will want us to serve Him in love, not in fear.

Anybody can tell the truth under duress. God does not use torture to extract a truth. He uses love instead.

If the scripture below had been obeyed in righteousness, maybe she would have lived. But the scripture was used in a negative manner.

1 Corinthians 1:10 "Now I beseech you, brethren, by the name our Lord Jesus Christ, that ye all speak the same thing, and that there be no divisions among you; but that ye be perfectly joined together in the same mind and the same judgment."

God is no respecter of persons.

Proverbs 11: 20-21 "They that are of a forward heart are abomination to the Lord: but such as upright in their way are his delight

21 Though hand joins in hand, the wicked shall not be unpunished: but the seed of the righteous shall be delivered."

We saw how a lie to Peter became a lie against the Holy Spirit. Be warned.

Don't be united with anybody in iniquity. The fact that you are joined together does not mean you must die together.

Be like ancient Lot and leave your spouse behind when it comes to disobeying God.

Can We Make These Declarations Together?

1. The union with my spouse will not lead to my untimely death in Jesus Name.
2. I am joined with my spouse for good, not for evil.
3. My family shall never be used as an example of an evil lesson.
4. Our service in the Kingdom shall not end in a tragedy.
5. We will not lose our rewards in Jesus Name, Amen.

Topic For Discussion

1. Who takes the blame, Mr or Mrs. Ananias?

"...with the Consent {full knowledge} of his wife sold the land."

CHAPTER 8

WHO IS IN YOUR KITCHEN?

2 Kings 4:38 "And Elisha came again to Gilgal: and there was a dearth in the land; and the sons of the prophets were sitting before him: and he said unto his servant, 'Set on the great pot, and seethe pottage for the sons of the prophets.'

39 And one went out into the field to gather herbs, and found a wild vine, and gathered thereof wild gourds his lap full, and came and shred them into the pot of pottage: for they knew them not.

40 So they poured out for the men to eat. And it came to pass, as they were eating of the pottage, that they cried out, and said, 'O thou man of God, there is death in the pot.' And they could not eat thereof.

41 But he said, 'Then bring meal.' And he cast it into the pot; and he said, 'Pour out for the people, that they may eat.' And there was no harm in the pot."

Friends, the above scriptures perfectly captured the event than anyone could imagine. 'DEATH IN THE POT.' We seemed to have more deaths in our pots today than any time in human history. The incidents of food poisoning are alarming.

The Centre For Disease Control And Prevention (CDC) of America found out that: "...of all the foodborne illnesses in the US, unspecified agents cause 38.4 million episodes of foodborne illnesses in the USA each year. 48 million people get sick, 128,000 are hospitalized, and 3,000 die from foodborne diseases each year in the US."
www.cdc.gov/foodbornburden/index.htm

I believe that the death toll could be much higher were it not for the high-tech medical facilities available in combating the menace.

Dearth in the Land

2 Kings 4:38 "...and there was a dearth in the land..."

This is not new you will say. When you have no farm or farming activities going on; what you then get is famine. This can be as a result of weather vagaries which might include excessive or inadequate rainfall, drought conditions, and so on.

The first culprit of famine is nutrition. And before long, the dearth in the land becomes death in the pot.

Elisha's visit to Gilgal was at the time the land was experiencing great famine. It was a tough time for the student prophets at the Gilgal School of Prophecy. There was no food anywhere. And of course, the herbs that survive during a famine are usually the poisonous ones. So when Prophet Elisha commanded that the big pot be set on the fire for a miraculous supply; one of the student prophets could not hide his excitement. He rushed straight into a nearby bush in search of herbs—edible veggies. But, instead of healthy herbs, the young prophet returned with his lap full of wild gourds. Here is how the Scripture described his action.

2 Kings 4:39 "And one went out into the field to gather herbs, and found a wild vine, and gathered thereof wild gourds his lap full, and came and shred them into the pot of pottage: for they knew them not."

The Ignorant Chef

The above scripture raises more questions than answers. A lot of things went wrong here. Yes, he wanted a delicious and nutritious meal for his colleagues. But he is ignorant. Such an assignment should have been safely carried out by the person who could differentiate between edible and poisonous herbs. The truth is that poisonous herbs must produce poisonous meals. A lot of our cooks today are kitchen illiterates. They have no idea about nutrition. They do not prepare the food: they only cook it. They are ignorant of the fact that foods are selected and prepared based on the required nutritional combination.

Any family with this kind of chef will most likely suffer from diverse nutritional deficiency. This might include an imminent food poisoning attack.

According to Premium Times, about 200,000 people die each year as a result of food poisoning in Nigeria. The truth is that most cases of food poisoning occur as a result of human activities.

What reason will make the student prophet not to separate the wild gourds from the edible ones? He does not see the need for such separation. In his ignorance, he thought the veggies were all good enough for the pottage.

But what about washing the leaves which is a normal kitchen routine practice. Will it be right to say that hunger makes people cut corners, even health corners? What do they get? Death in the pot.

2 Kings 4:39 "...gathered thereof wild gourds his lap full, and came and shred them into the pot of pottage..."

Friends, when your kitchen is run in this manner: death will certainly find its way into your pot.

This death is worst in some developing countries where you have prolonged famine due to conflicts, drought, and even natural disasters. People sacrifice nutrients and hygiene on the altar of hunger.

The Agency Report of Wednesday the 1st of March 2017, alarmed that "...in Kano, about 55,000 children were treated for acute malnutrition in 2016, of the 397,515 estimated to be acutely malnourished." This I call 'non-pathogenic self-poisoning.'

www.premiumtimesng.com/News

Public Restaurants Are Also Guilty

Some of the health challenges we have these days are as a result of unhealthy and irresponsible kitchen practices. This is commonly observed in some of our public restaurants and where few people care. These care-free behaviors exist in spite of government regulations. This is, therefore, more of an attitude thing. That is why even those with certificates violate basic healthy kitchen practices when cooking. It is worse for lazy people. Most lazy people are careless. They don't have the time to be thorough.

A lot of restaurant operators fell into the temptation of choosing 'TASTE' at the expense of 'HEALTH' especially when profit is the central goal. The cook wants your praise at the end of the meal. He wouldn't want you to know that 'tasty meals does not mean 'healthy' meals. You must part with the money in your pocket with joy and 'satisfaction.'

Ask yourself this question.

IF PEOPLE KNOW HOW YOU PREPARED YOUR MEALS WOULD THEY EAT THEM?

A member of my staff once told me a story of what happened in a restaurant near our place of work. This vibrant restaurant was the choice of many because of their price and how delicious their meals were. Located on a construction site, the customers were mostly site workers.

One fateful afternoon, the restaurant was packed full of people. The waiters were not finding it easy to meet up with the volume of orders placed at the same time by these hungry costumers. Everyone was mindful of the break time and wanted to go back to their office on time.

The restaurant proprietor has a child in kindergarten who usually comes back by this time of the day. On arrival from school, this boy was observed urinating into a freshly prepared soup pot.

Before she knew what was happening, the news had gone round. Those who were still standing walked out without waiting for their meals. That was how the restaurant closed down. No one wanted to go and eat 'urine soup.'

That was an accident, but who cares. Here is another question. If that accident happened when nobody was around, will the woman throw away the soup? This is why you should be in charge of your meals as much as you can. A lot of things happen in the kitchen.

Yes, you don't have to be a professional nutritionist to make healthy meals for your family. But we all need to have the basic knowledge of food types and how they affect our body.

Books such as "**The Healthiest People On Earth Cookbook**" written by Joy M. Neufeld and Carrie Wachsmann, and "**Aging Without Growing Old**" written by Judy Lindberg with Laura Gladys McFarland can provide immense cooking and dietary assistance.

Those who cannot read and write like my grandmother should take some practical lessons from those who know better. There is no disputing the fact that most natural and locally made traditional meals made by them rates high on the modern nutritional scale.

The Kitchen as a Home Clinic

The kitchen is more than a place where food is prepared for hungry folks. It is like a home laboratory where critical health condiments are formulated.

In a testimony published by Joy M. Neufeld and Carrie Wachsmann in their book, *The Healthiest People on Earth Cookbook*, Don and Joy Neufeld testified as follows:

"In 1990, my husband Don was diagnosed as diabetic Type 2; which is adult onset diabetes. He kept it under control with medication and diet for a few years. In 1996, he was having an awful time keeping his sugar under control. Then we heard about a new way of eating which would help to control the sugar. We decided to try this way of cooking. Within a week of eating the natural, healthy way as outlined in their book, his sugar came down to a normal healthy level..."

From the above testimony, it was obvious that the kitchen was the Clinic.

This famous quote:

"*Let Food Be Thy Medicine and Medicine Be Thy Food*" by Hippocrates (460BC-377BC), who is regarded as the father of medicine and the greatest physician of his time lives with us today.

For me, this is the basis for preventive medicine. Every public health campaign should start in the home kitchen.

Apart from cooking to eat and eating to live, other things such as kitchen hygiene should be taken seriously.

A healthy kitchen translates to a healthy home. Hence, kitchen hygiene should be the responsibility of every member of the family. Don't wait until death is found in your pot. That may be very disastrous. It might lead to something you may not be able to handle.

"Elisha" may not be available on such days for a quick fix.

Now, as I was writing, a sad announcement of a cholera outbreak in one of the state's High schools (name withheld) came over the radio. Over a thousand students according to the broadcast had been hospitalized. I pray for their speedy recovery.

Meanwhile, the agencies concerned are reviewing the hygienic condition of the school, the kitchen being the first port of call. Now we know that the home is as healthy as its kitchen.

1 Samuel 30:11-12 "And they found an Egyptian in the field, and brought him to David, and gave him bread, and he did eat; and they made him drink water; And they gave him a piece of a cake of figs, and two clusters of raisins: and when he had eaten, his spirit came again to him: for he had eaten no bread, nor drunk any water, three days and three nights."

Here is what happened. On interrogation, the young man said:

1 Samuel 30:13 "...I am a young man of Egypt, servant to an Amalekite; and my master left me, because three days agone I fell sick."

The Egyptian in the above scriptures was not rushed to the emergency section of a local hospital. The greatest need of his life this time was not the pills but a healthy kitchen product. The fuel his body needed to drive his spirit and soul was used up. The spirit was almost saying goodbye to the body when they found him. "...his spirit came again to him..." the Bible said.

In our world today, millions of people are in similar conditions. Their lives are gradually coming to a halt. We must all behave like David who for a while, halted all his pursuit to provide the required need for this dying 'enemy' of his.

People are starving in the midst of plenty all over the world. This situation is worsened every day by civil wars, corruption, famine and so. The politicians are not helping matters. Looting can be found everywhere. The world must rise to help our starving brothers and sisters.

Don't be Callous, Feed the People Under Your Care

God expects us to provide food and nourishment for those He puts under our care. The scripture below is about a virtuous woman.

Proverbs 31:14-15 "She is like the trading-ships, getting food from far away. She gets up while it is still night, and gives meat to her family, and their food to her servant-girls."

But who says we cannot be a virtuous President, a virtuous Director or even a virtuous Army Commander. God takes care of people using people. In this case, leaders are most suitable.

Verse sixteen of first Samuel 30 graphically portrays the attitude of most leaders today.

I want to think that this abandoned young Egyptian man was a military officer attached to one of the raiding Commanders. He had been very active during their previous Military operations.

Hear what he said to David:

1 Samuel 30:14 "We made an invasion upon the south of the Cherethites, and upon the coast which belongeth to Judah, and upon the south of Caleb, and we burned Ziklag with fire."

But his Commanders prefer to dance around the spoils while their subjects starved and wasted away in sickness.

1 Samuel 30:16 "...behold, they were spread abroad upon all the earth, eating and drinking, and dancing, because of all the great spoil that they had taken out of the land of the Philistines, and out of the land of Judah."

This Amalekite dance did not last for too long. The abandoned, Egyptian young man was now leading the victorious army for a complete recovery. This was God in action, made possible after a recovery meal was administered.

This does not mean you should worship good meals. God should be the one using the healthy meals to keep you healthy, rather than the meals using God. Anything not done in faith is sin the Bible says. So bless your meals and eat them by faith.

Cook With Revelation, Let God be your Nutritionist

Daniel 1:11

"Then said Daniel to Melzar, whom the prince of the eunuchs had set over Daniel, Hananiah, Mishael, and Azariah,

12 Prove thy servants, I beseech thee, ten days; and let them give us pulse to eat, and water to drink.

13 Then let our countenances be looked upon before thee, and the countenance of the children that eat of the portion of the king's meat: and as thou seest, deal with thy servants.

14 So he consented to them in this matter, and proved them ten days.

15 And at the end of ten days, their countenances appeared fairer and fatter in the flesh than all the children which did eat the portion of the king's meat."

The story of these Hebrew children in Daniel chapter one was a clear act of God. The three-year nourishment program and training would not be necessary. What was required was the right but anointed meal.

The Persian nutritionists were helpless and further mesmerized by He who formed the human body. God's menu, though simple, cheap and easy to prepare was unbeatable. It produced a three-year result in 10 days. What a mighty God we serve.

But what was this wonder meal that has everything the body required? It is called "**PULSE** and **WATER.**" Some other translations called it "**Vegetables** and **Water.**"

Daniel 1:12 "Please test your servants for ten days and let us be given vegetables to eat and water to drink" (ISV)

PULSE, according to *The Advanced English Dictionary*, refers to "Edible seeds of various pod-bearing plants." This might include peas, beans, lentils, etc. All vegetable-based foods.

This cannot, of course, be compared in any way to the 'elitist poison' we eat today in the name of refined foods.

Daniel may not have had any knowledge on Food Technology and Nutrition. He had one knowledge that must never be compromised. Not even in the face of free federal meals allocated to them in the palace. And that one knowledge is the knowledge of God of Israel.

Daniel 1:15 "At the end of ten days their

appearance was better and their faces were well-nourished compared to the young men who ate the King's rich food." (ISV)

Notice that the Bible described the formulated King's food as rich too. But that obviously couldn't have been as natural and rich as Daniel's meal. The evidence was clear. "...their appearance was better and their faces were well-nourished compared to the young men who ate the King's rich food."

Now we know that God is concerned with what we eat. Let us be very careful about the things we allow into our body: the temple of the living God.

My prayer for your homes is in this:

May God satisfy your homes with good things and cause your family to be renewed like the Eagles in Jesus Name.

Psalm 103:5 "Who satisfieth thy mouth with good things; so that thy youth is renewed like the eagle's."

Here is a piece of advice from Isaiah the prophet which could guide our homes and kitchens.

Isaiah 55:2 "Why pay money for something that will not nourish you? Why spend your hard-earned money on something that will not satisfy? Listen carefully to me and eat what is nourishing! Enjoy fine food!" (NET)

There will be no death in your pot from henceforth; rather your pot will be full of life in Jesus' Name.

CHAPTER 9

THE EGO OF HEROD AND THE STRENGTH OF A WOMAN

Mark 6:17-28

"For Herod himself had sent forth and laid hold upon John, and bound him in prison for Herodias' sake, his brother Philip's wife: for he had married her.

18 For John had said unto Herod, It is not lawful for thee to have thy brother's wife.

19 Therefore Herodias had a quarrel against him, and would have killed him; but she could not:

20 For Herod feared John, knowing that he was a just man and an holy, and observed him; and when he heard him, he did many things, and heard him gladly.

21 And when a convenient day was come, that Herod on his birthday made a supper to his lords, high captains, and chief estates of Galilee;

22 And when the daughter of the said Herodias came in, and danced, and pleased Herod and them that sat with him, the king said unto the damsel,

Ask of me whatsoever thou wilt, and I will give it thee.

23 And he sware unto her, Whatsoever thou shalt ask of me, I will give it thee, unto the half of my kingdom.

24 And she went forth, and said unto her mother, What shall I ask? And she said, The head of John the Baptist.

25 And she came in straightway with haste unto the king, and asked, saying, I will that thou give me by and by in a charger the head of John the Baptist.

26 And the king was exceeding sorry; yet for his oath's sake, and for their sakes, which sat with him, he would not reject her.

27 And immediately the king sent an executioner, and commanded his head to be brought: and he went and beheaded him in the prison,

28 And brought his head in a charger, and gave it to the damsel: and the damsel gave it to her mother. "

Genesis 40:20-22

"And it came to pass the third day, which was Pharaoh's birthday, that he made a feast unto all his servants: and he lifted up the head of the chief butler and of the chief baker among his servants.

21 And he restored the chief butler unto his butlership again, and he gave the cup into Pharaoh's hand:

22 But he hanged the chief baker: as Joseph had interpreted to them."

Friends, if I propose a ban against birthday celebrations, will you support me? Well, you don't have to anymore. I have a better understanding of those Scriptures now, than when I first encountered them. I have taken a new position. And that is:

1. Herod's birthday was a death day. And so I must make sure mine would be a life-giving day. Reaching out to save life for the Lord Jesus.

2. Herod's birthday was a display of Pride, Ego, and Impunity. But mine should manifest Humility, Love, and Appreciation to God.

3. Herod's birthday was a day of vengeance and manipulation. But mine should be a day to forgive people and make my life straight for the Lord.

4. At Herod's birthday, satan was glorified as Truth was sacrificed on the altar of Ego. But, my birthday must be a day to disgrace Satan and the truth upheld in righteousness.

5. It was a day of careless utterance after a demonic dance. I will bless the Lord and sing spiritual song to Him for the gift of life.

You see why I stopped blaming God for not sending a thunderstorm to kill his Excellency and scatter his devil-ridden birthday celebration. The Scripture below is a consolation as it explains the reason for such impunity.

Ecclesiastes 8:11 "Because sentence against an evil work is not executed speedily, therefore the heart of the sons of men is fully set in them to do evil".

Herod As A Family Man

There could be someone out there who shares a similar experience with his Excellency, Herod Antipas that the My prayer is that the Lord will miraculously put this book in the hands of such a person. Beloved, let not the mention of Herod make you lose interest in the above subject matter or even provoke you in any way. Most people don't want to read about him due to his callous behavior. In this context, we are looking at him as a family man, just like you and I.

Most prominent personalities in our society today have only one problem. Sure your innocent mind wouldn't be thinking of money, power, position, and so on. That of course, made them prominent in the first place. So you are right in your thinking.

However, the one problem that is common among them is marital problem. Marital problems do not recognize dignitaries. It has no respect to personalities. It dehumanizes the most powerful and ridicules the most respected. These days, we watch with dismay the marital struggles amongst our rulers world over. Just like Herod, it has been one nasty story after another. In certain quarters, a new position attracts a new and befitting wife. This in most cases translates to new and unbefitting family trouble. All these were as a result of human Ego.

Ego Defined

The Advanced English Dictionary defined Ego as "An inflated feeling of pride in your superiority to others."

This inflated feeling of pride is always associated with power and position. They have the feeling that they can do and undo. Ego is the pride of position. It gives voice and expression to pride.

Ego, as far as I am concerned, is a 'Position Virus.' They are viruses associated with positions. It is fundamentally a man's disease. Just being a man makes you vulnerable if God does not help you. Women also manifest this virus when they come to positions of authority. Some Advanced Countries are now using human right and equality Laws to curtail it. Unfortunately, there were no such campaigns in Herod's time.

The only religious law available was violated with impunity. Jewish laws does not permit a man to marry his niece.

Leviticus 20:21 "And if a man shall take his brother's wife, it is an unclean thing: he hath uncovered his brother's nakedness; they shall be childless".

Leviticus 18:16 "Thou shalt not uncover the nakedness of thy brother's wife: it is thy brother's nakedness"

They make irrational statements when they are 'high'. They make euphemistic speeches that are egocentric. They make promises in order to show their superiority to others. They make promises to the half of their Kingdoms. God hates it. He killed one of them in Acts chapter twelve.

Acts 12:21-23 "And upon a set day Herod, arrayed in royal apparel, sat upon his throne, and made an oration unto them. And the people gave a shout, saying, It is the voice of a god, and not of a man. And immediately the angel of the Lord smote him, because he gave not God the glory: and he was eaten of worms, and gave up the ghost."

Ego in Some Cultures

Some men run their home based on certain cultures and traditions. They relegate their wives to the background making them feel inferior to the society. They come up with a long list of the things that are forbidden for women.

The men want to show superiority over the women. They see women as agents of defilement and as such must not be allowed to enter certain places. Men are the ones in high favour with the gods. Women are not to have any say in the community. In certain traditions, if a man falls down in the course of any squabble with his woman; he will not rise up from the ground until the woman provides a cock.

Even some Christian men are still struggling with these unscriptural trado-christian lifestyles in the church. All these are as a result of the "Ego of man". But thank God for the light of the Gospel and for civilization.

The truth is that Ego does not recognize gender. It is satanic and as such can operate anywhere irrespective of your gender classification.

Unfortunately, the church is not spared. Those who are called to lead find themselves battling with the same Ego. Ego does not allow the junior to correct the senior.

It places one above rebuke, making one believe he knows it all. Ego has a blinding effect. It makes one ignore certain danger signs and signals. The only thing imminent is a fall. And the Bible says how great is such a fall. Indeed, Ego has blinding effects.

I have on several occasions observed responsible and tongues- speaking brethren misfire when it comes to marriages. I will never forget one such experience. This opened my eyes and I saw how dangerous Ego can be.

During my college days, I was elected as one of the executive members of a Campus Christian Fellowship. Our executive team included a very committed and faithful sister who occupied the position of a prayer coordinator. She was like God's spokesperson in the fellowship and a prayer warrior too. Many of us wanted to be like her. I personally asked her (just like Jesus' disciples) to teach me how to pray. I was sincerely willing to be her disciple. She was not the gentle and soft type. Everyone knew her on the campus for her faith.

On this fateful day, I was scornfully invited to come and watch my sister in action. My fear was if the boys had beaten her for sharing the Gospel with them. I got there reluctantly. But brethren, I couldn't believe my eyes. One of the unbelievers who was always against the fellowship and against everything God had become her boyfriend. When she saw me she joined them to make jest of me and the fellowship. Could this ever happened, you may ask? Yes, it happened publicly.

In fact, the picture was like a public declaration into a new party usually made during a political rally by political juggernauts during which a decampee denounces his loyalty to his previous political party.

I had sleepless nights and lost my appetite for two weeks. I was looking for who will tell me that what I had just watched was a movie clip and nothing to worry about. You can imagine what was going on in my young Christian mind. I became apprehensive. Could this be how all of us will end? My mind was bombarded with questions and more questions, with no answer in view. It looked like all of us were fake.

The worst was when she returned all the fellowship material in her possession without saying a word to anyone. The following day she asked me to return all her books and have nothing to do with her anymore. The drama was just refusing to come to an end.

Well, what looked like the end, was that she ended up marrying that man. Yes, I mean marrying that man. A man that was parading himself like the 'Anti-Christ' on the campus. She graduated before us and went away with her newly-found husband. Ego made her think we were too small to correct her, and as far as she was concerned she knew it all.

Herodias: The Boss Behind The Scene

It is foolishness to underrate the strength of any woman. Unfortunately, men play the fool most of the time. They don't realize that when a woman swallows a matter, it doesn't get to her belly. It stays somewhere in her heart. So It will be logical to stay out of the way of such ladies until the matter gets to her stomach where digestion will probably take place.

Mark 6:18 -19 "For John had said unto Herod, It is not lawful for thee to have thy brother's wife. Therefore Herodias had a quarrel against him, and would have killed him; but she could not..."

Mark 6:21 "And when a convenient day was come…"

The above scriptures should be a lesson for all. This is because most women don't believe a matter is over until it is all over. So study your spouse and go to God in prayer if you discover any Herodias tendencies.

A local adage in my hometown says " When a woman welcomes you in her home: look at her face twice before making a decision to stay overnight despite her husband's invitation." Women are powerful. They can make positive influence for the Lord. On the other hand, it is usually disastrous when such powers are operated under the influence of satan.

Jezebel was outstanding. Though a typical example of a heathen spouse, but the spirit is still exerting her influence in the willing minds of some Christian folks.

1 Kings 21:5-6 "But Jezebel his wife came to him, and said unto him, Why is thy spirit so sad, that thou eatest no bread? And he said unto her, Because I spake unto Naboth the Jezreelite, and said unto him, Give me thy vineyard for money; or else, if it please thee, I will give thee another vineyard for it: and he answered, I will not give thee my vineyard. And Jezebel his wife said unto him, Dost thou now govern the kingdom of Israel? arise, and eat bread, and let thine heart be merry: I will give thee the vineyard of Naboth the Jezreelite."

Ahab the king failed in his negotiation with Naboth. But her Excellency said **"I will give thee the vineyard of Naboth the Jezreelite"**. And she delivered in her promise. Jezebel spirit has no regard for inheritance. Spiritual personalities means nothing to them as we see in chapter nineteen of first kings.

1 Kings 19:1-2 "And Ahab told Jezebel all that Elijah had done, and withal how he had slain all the prophets with the sword. 2 Then Jezebel sent a messenger unto Elijah, saying, So let the gods do to me, and more also, if I make not thy life as the life of one of them by tomorrow about this time."

A woman under the spirit of jealousy can pull down a kingdom in seconds not minding how long it took to build it. Head of prophet Elijah? She must be joking. But that was exactly what she wanted. The gods have been involved by an irrevocable oath.

"So let the gods do to me, and more also, if I make not thy life as the life of one of them by to-morrow about this time."

These days it is not uncommon to hear some wives speak the same way. I have seen ministries crumble, ministers resigning their calling and godly homes set ablaze under the burning rage of a jealous woman. So husbands, be careful with that kingdom emissary in your house not to provoke her to jealousy. She is on assignment to do you good. That is the idea of God giving you "an help meet" the type of help you require.

Genesis 2:18 "And the LORD God said, It is not good that the man should be alone; I will make him an help meet for him."

A natural and unregenerated woman can give you hell or help depending on which one you can handle. This same woman at new birth is recreated to an enviable vessel in the hand of the Lord for the good of any man.

Vital Points
As a husband, don't rule your home with irrational and impulsive promises

Such promises to the half of your kingdom can only be withdrawn when you have no woman to enforce it. You may have made such mistake when you were wooing her. It shouldn't follow you into the marriage. Be realistic with your spouse. Avoid ambiguous and unfulfillable party speeches. This can erode your integrity quotient in the heart of your spouse.

The consequence of such speeches are usually unbearable. Please dear reader, take time to go through the scriptures below.

Ask yourself the following questions:

1. What are your likes and dislikes about the characters found in this passage?
2. What do you think was the role of God and man as observed?

What other personal lessons are there for you to learn?

Judges 11:30-40

"And Jephthah vowed a vow unto the LORD, and said, If thou shalt without fail deliver the children of Ammon into mine hands,

31 Then it shall be, that whatsoever cometh forth of the doors of my house to meet me, when I return in peace from the children of Ammon, shall surely be the LORD's, and I will offer it up for a burnt offering.

32 So Jephthah passed over unto the children of Ammon to fight against them, and the LORD delivered them into his hands.

33 And he smote them from Aroer, even till thou come to Minnith, even twenty cities, and unto the plain of the vineyards, with a very great slaughter.

Thus the children of Ammon were subdued before the children of Israel.

34 And Jephthah came to Mizpeh unto his house, and, behold, his daughter came out to meet him with timbrels and with dances: and she was his only child; beside her, he had neither son nor daughter.

35 And it came to pass, when he saw her, that he rent his clothes, and said, Alas, my daughter! thou hast brought me very low, and thou art one of them that trouble me: for I have opened my mouth unto the LORD, and I cannot go back.

36 And she said unto him, My father, if thou hast opened thy mouth unto the LORD, do to me according to that which hath proceeded out of thy mouth; forasmuch as the LORD hath taken vengeance for thee of thine enemies, even of the children of Ammon.

37 And she said unto her father, Let this thing be done for me: let me alone two months, that I may go up and down upon the mountains, and bewail my virginity, I and my fellows.

38 And he said, Go. And he sent her away for two months: and she went with her companions, and bewailed her virginity upon the mountains.

39 And it came to pass at the end of two months, that she returned unto her father, who did with her according to his vow which he had vowed: and she knew no man. And it was a custom in Israel,

40 That the daughters of Israel went yearly to lament the daughter of Jephthah the Gileadite four days in a year."

We can, therefore, establish the following truths:

1. Men should always learn to face the truth than struggling to save their faces in Ego.

For Herod, the truth is that he should not marry his niece. But he was bent on saving his face from shame.

2. Death is averted whenever a truth revealed is practiced.

Don't allow the devil to be smarter than you. Make a quick turn. Don't allow him to highjack that situation.

3. To promise and fail is better than keeping a demon-motivated promise.

Don't be the devils' advocate. Stop when you notice it was his speech and summon up the courage to turn around. Don't go ahead in managing the error. Life errors are difficult to manage. During my secondary school days, we were told that errors are better managed and eliminated at the beginning of the experiment than the end of it. So it is better to stop that relationship now, rather than a divorce after the birth of your first child.

Who is in Control, Herod or the devil?

It is obvious that the devil stole the show using the following means:

His Ego (Yet for his Oath's sake)

You will realize that most people fulfill an evil promise backed up by evil oath not because they fear the gods but because of their Ego.

Mark 6:26 "And the king was exceeding sorry; yet for his oath's sake, and for their sakes which sat with him, he would not reject her."

The Bible said, "the king was exceeding sorry." Meaning he was deeply regretful. He was in pain. His entire being was against the request before him. But for his Ego, he acted otherwise.

I have heard women interject emphatically during some of my counseling sessions. They say: "Pastor you don't know my husband. He is a man of his word. He doesn't change his position even if the heavens are falling." Some other ladies said: "Pastor, except God, no one can change my husband's position not even the Angels." I inquired to know if that was a mere figure of speech, and they said no.

Dear reader, what most people call integrity today is mere expression of Ego. Integrity does not mean one holding blindly to his wrong and harmful positions just because he has given his words and would not want to be seen as dishonest. If I may suggest. A man of integrity, is that man with the ability to change when he discovers that his positions and promises are wrong, ungodly and inhuman to be fulfilled.

The Public (..and for their sakes who sat with him)

This is usually the problem with public figures. They build their lives around their colleagues. They make life unbearable for their family members at home. Their homes are governed by public opinions. Everything is "...**for their sakes which sat with him.**" This puts the entire family on a lifelong drilling exercise.

Even the pastors are not spared. Their families operate under pressure. They must live as little gods, far above mistakes and failure. The church folks set the standard which they must comply with. They are hunted daily by such words as: "and you call yourself a pastors child or wife" No one remembers that God only called the pastor. His household is just an extension of his flock.

His Strange Wife, Herodias.

She was an opportunist. She pulled the trigger when the stage was set. "**..therefore Herodias had a quarrel against him, and would have killed him; but she could not.....and when a convenient day was come..**"

It could have been a covenant day to bless the man of God and not to ask for his head. You that suggests evil to your husband, repent. Save your husband from shading Innocent blood.

The Devil.

The devil obviously drew the plan. The script was acted out perfectly. Unfortunately, the devil was never seen seated at the party. But he silently directed the affairs of the celebrants. He will do the same if you grant him a place in your family. The choice is yours.

MY PRAYER FOR YOUR FAMILY IS:

1. Your home will not be like the one described above, in Jesus Name.
2. Your home will be ruled by the eternal word of God.
3. Your home will always seek for occasion to bless not to kill.
4. You will be the help your husband requires.
5. Your happy moments will not end up in tragedy.
6. Your home will be rid of guilt, and no nasty story will surround your marriage in Jesus Mighty Name Amen.

CHAPTER 10

THE BLACK BOX IN MARRIAGE

Merriam-Webster Dictionaries defines a black box as a complicated electronic device whose internal mechanism is usually hidden or mysterious to the user. Webster maintains that it is a "Crashworthy Device" in aircraft for recording cockpit conversations and flight data."

You get to hear about it in event of a crash. It is not a safety device. As a matter of fact, it is not useful during safe flight. It is fitted and used in most large planes should there be a crash.

Without further sounding like an Aeronaut, one will say that God seemed to have this 'Crash Appliance' installed in every home to record the cockpit conversations and the flight data as husband and wife journey together. The Lord confirms this in the writing of Apostle Luke.

Luke 12: 2-3 "But there is nothing covered up, that shall not be revealed, and hid, that shall not be known. So, whatever you have said in the dark, will come to men's hearing in the light, and what you have said secretly inside the house, will be made public from the house-tops."

Wow! Does the above Scripture not sound as if a recording device was planted around His disciples? Of course yes! It is high time God's children come to terms with the above truth. This understanding will positively impact your life and the relationship with your spouse.

God is Omniscient. He is the Unseen One who sees and knows everything. Nothing is hidden from His sight. God dwells in utter brightness. And the Bible said, "in Him, there is no darkness at all." No one can play hide and seek games before Him. He is transparent, open and plain. He wants His children to operate with the same spirit. He exposes anyone who involves in cover-ups and hypocrisies.

Unfortunately, spouses keep all manner of secrets to themselves. They lie to one another about many things. Others who don't want to lie, keep things quiet and secret. To continuously cover up a matter, one will requires newer versions of old lies as the case may be. There are many things your spouse doesn't know about you. You covered it up during the first year. And now, many years have passed and you think it is all forgotten and over.

Well, I am sorry to inform you that it is not over yet.

God will definitely expose these secrets. I am not wishing you evil. The truth is that nobody likes a rooftop exposure were the so-called secrets are made public for the world to see. When we allow that to happens, the outcome is usually a 'matrimonial crash'. The oneness is lost and most marriages don't survive it. Very few people go to their graves with their secrets hidden, and you may not be lucky enough to be one of those.

This is what prophet Isaiah said:

Isaiah 29:15 "Woe unto them that seek deep to hide their counsel from the LORD, and their works are in the dark, and they say, Who seeth us? and who knoweth us?"

Couples do all manners of things to themselves. Some act like a detective on a fact-finding mission in the home of a suspect. Others behave as though they came for a four-month parental posting, after which they return to their parent for more tutorials. For God's sake, you are not on Industrial Attachment or Internship. Marriage is meant to last 'forever'. The earlier we believe this, the more committed we will be to our relationship. Trust, openness, determination and more are required to make it happen.

Financial Secrets

When you love money instead of your spouse, a lot of things happen. The relationship will not cover a distance before a crash. Few days are required for its total collapse. It means evil, and in fact, all evil will have taken root in your family. Here is a warning from Apostle Paul:

1 Timothy 6:10 "For the love of money is the root of all evil: which while some coveted after, they have erred from the faith, and pierced themselves through with many sorrows."

There are things you must not do in order to avoid "piercing yourselves through with many sorrows."

Avoid certain financial misbehaviors such as:

1. Operating a Secret Account

Financial openness should, as a matter of fact, be adopted as one of the cardinal policies at home. Some women believe that how much they earn and where they keep such money is nobody's business. My sister, you will soon discover that it is even more of your spouse's business than yours. When he gets to know of these financials secrets –which will definitely happen- you will not be happy with the outcome.

Some men believe that their position as a husband is bastardized the day their wives get to know what they earn. I am still wondering how men can believe this. The men in this group believe that wives will become irrational and increase their demands.

One man told me that the moment a woman sees the bottom of your pocket, that pocket will develop holes in less than one month. He said the holes get wider as the days go by. The shopping lists are constantly revised and expanded. And when you ask if they are listed in their order of importance, she will say no and rather maintain that all the items are very necessary just that they cannot appear as item one on the list all at the same time.

If you tell them your wife is not like that, they will call you a blessed man. I know some women could be tough. But we cannot generalize this lifestyle for every woman. In fact, never for the Christian woman. A Christian woman understands the concept of oneness in marriage. She has nothing to hide. They belong to each other.

The book of Ephesians explained it properly.

Ephesians 5:31 "For this cause shall a man leave his father and mother, and shall be joined unto his wife, and they two shall be one flesh."

It is an error and a misplacement for one spouse to hide things from the other. So I don't believe that the hole in your pocket was bored by your wife. In the book of Haggai, we see what the Prophet said could perforate a man's bag, especially if he is a child of God.

Haggai 1:3-4 & 6 "Then came the word of the LORD by Haggai the prophet, saying, Is it time for you, O ye, to dwell in your ceiled houses, and this house lie waste?"

Verse six spells out the consequences.

Haggai 1:6 "Ye have sown much, and bring in little; ye eat, but ye have not enough; ye drink, but ye are not filled with drink; ye clothe you, but there is none warm; and he that earneth wages earneth wages to put it into a bag with holes."

The above scripture sounds like a complete shutdown of all your income gates and resources. It must not be allowed to happen.

Another scripture to watch is:

Malachi 3:8,10 &11 " Will a man rob God? Yet ye have robbed me. But ye say, Wherein have we robbed thee? In tithes and offerings. Bring ye all the tithes into the storehouse, that there may be meat in mine house, and prove me now herewith, saith the LORD of hosts, if I will not open you the windows of heaven, and pour you out a blessing, that there shall not be room enough to receive it. And I will rebuke the devourer for your sakes, and he shall not destroy the fruits of your ground; neither shall your vine cast her fruit before the time in the field, saith the LORD of hosts."

This is suitable, isn't it? This is like identifying a problem and attaching the solution.

There are other things that can perforate a man's pocket. These include reckless spending, lack of planning and budgeting, living above your means, etc.

2. Secret Expenses

This can lead to a serious crisis at home, depending on the type of financial policy one operates. In all, openness is the key. Keep it open, if you have nothing to hide. My wife reports back to me irrespective of who brings in the cash. And because she keeps me in the picture, I don't have to ask questions such as: "How do you manage? What happened to the money?" and so on. These questions are common among men, especially when what is budgeted for the month suddenly ends up being spent before the month is half over. We should also recognize the man, as the head of the family, will naturally require some level of accountability from the spouse. He is by default, the Chief Executive Officer. This does not, however, mean undue scrutiny of her shopping lists.

3. Secret Business Deals

Some spouses are fond of engaging in secret business deals. Some couples have been destroyed by this practice. Others incur heavy financial losses and thereafter plunge the entire family into unbearable financial affliction. They admit their error only when they had their fingers burnt.

The Bible said two are better than one. Two good heads you will say. Of course yes, but mind you we are talking about God's children. My father in the Lord, Dr. John Akpami once said: "No one born of

God can be described as a monster, because God's chromosomes are in him."

If it is God who gave you your partner, you can be sure of good Counsel from each other. "Never!" you say. What does he or she know about business? Business is about ideas and strategies and has little or nothing to do with gender.

The key is allowing the better manager to be the financial consultant for the home, irrespective of the person's gender. So share that business idea with each other and take it to God in prayer.

4. Shoddy Transactions

This includes those transactions that are not pure in the eyes of God. Amongst such are, secret professional misconduct. These range across medical, legal, and social practitioners including the military. Some have innocently, but secretly purchased stolen goods and tarnished the image and reputation of the family. Your partner will be shocked when the law enforcement agents come after you. Your spouse declares you innocent with an oath before the officers, only to discover afterward that you are a culprit. What an embarrassing disappointment. Very few families recover from such a crisis.

Some have sold their houses without the knowledge of their wives. The family members get to know about the deal when the buyer comes with a quit or removal notice. What a shame.

For God's sake, you are first a child of God. Seeking a second opinion at such times from your spouse might open up a door of escape, thereby aborting the enemy's plans to disgrace your family.

5. Secret Loan Facility Unknown To The Family

Friends, creditors have no respect for persons. King David in the book of Psalms knows what they can do. He asked God to employ their services against his enemies when he said:

Psalms 109: 11 "May creditors seize all his possession, and may foreigners loot the property he has acquired." (ISV)

Can you Imagine a creditor, accompanied by law enforcement agents, unknown to your family, arriving at your home with a court order to seize your property, all in the name of debt recovery? The men are often caught in this trap even though they may have their reasons. But the question is "Why must it be a secret?" Open and transparent reasons are more easily understood.

Most creditors seemed to be more interested in the seizure than in the repayment. They don't accept death as debt cancellation. This was the case of the widowed wife of the student prophet in 2 Kings Four.

2 Kings 4:1 "Now there cried a certain woman of the wives of the sons of the prophets unto Elisha, saying, Thy servant my husband is dead, and thou knowest that thy servant did fear the LORD: and the creditor is come to take unto him my two sons to be bondmen."

To take away her two sons? Because of what, and for how much? But this is a common practice among creditors such as Banks, Mortgage Institutions, and Individual lending organizations world over. They have no piety for the dead, much less the living. They come to seize and to auction.

Imagine a scenario where the widow woman was not aware of the debt. She would swear to the heavens and the earth defending her husband. Some have fainted the moment the creditor tenders convincing evidence of the transaction. Those who survived, woke up to curse the day they met their late husband. The result is: the rich continue to rule over the poor, while the borrower continues to be a servant to the lender.

Proverbs 22:7 "The rich ruleth over the poor, and the borrower is servant to the lender."

Secret debt at the time of death is like 'evil parting gift' to the family. **Proverbs 13:22** says: "A good man Leaveth an inheritance to his Children's children." **NOT DEBT.**

6. Property Secrets

Property disputes are more common now than ever before. Property litigation solicitors are having it rough meeting up with the numerous and diverse kinds of property disputes that abound. Day by day relatives, siblings, and wives drag themselves to court due to property disputes.

Litigation, especially over land matters is usually expensive and takes a long time to resolve. Thank God for the process called Mediations using Alternative Dispute Resolution ADR mechanism. This method of dispute resolution reduces the length of time required to resolve a dispute. The beauty of this method is that the outcome is usually a win-win situation where relationships are restored in the end.

In spite of the above situations, couples further complicate the solicitor's jobs by keeping property secret. And because secrets are only known by the gods; resolving it is an uphill task with the humans.

In most cases, the disputes are left behind for the children to resolve, God knows how. There were cases where the devil used a dispute over one plot of land to wipe out an entire family pedigree. This is not fair in all its ramifications. Spouses must do their best to put their homes in order when everyone is around, knowing that you cannot respond to a court summons from the grave. If you won't listen to anyone, please listen to God. His counsel is simple: "Set Thine House In Order."

2 Kings 20:1 "In those days was Hezekiah sick unto death. And the prophet Isaiah the son of Amoz came to him, and said unto him, Thus saith the LORD, SET THINE HOUSE IN ORDER; for thou shalt die, and not live."

I heard a story of a man who rented his wife's

property for years without knowing it actually belonged to his wife. The deal was arranged through an agent who said the Landlord wouldn't want a direct dealing with the tenants. Smart wife you say. Hmmm! The question is, how long will this smartness last. But remember our anchor scripture in **Luke 12: 2-3** "But there is nothing covered up, that shall not be revealed..."

The worst thing was that this woman continued to increase the rent annually. One of the years, the husband struggled with the rent that he took out a loan in order to meet the rent obligation. His wife knew this and even encouraged him to go for the loan. Do you still call this smart? I pray it may never happen to you.

Well, a day came for the fulfillment of **Luke 12:2**, and the man vowed never to live under the same roof with such a woman. The woman should marry the house, right? Of course, that was the end of the marriage. It became a rooftop story all over the town. Her night came up at noonday. She crash landed beyond repairs. The only thing she left behind was this story.

7. Plan 'B' as a Reason

Often, spouses give different reasons for their secrecy. Some complain of extravagant husbands. Others point their fingers at a demanding wife. And the blame game continues like a swinging pendulum.

A lady once shared her experience with me during

one of my seminar sessions. She was building a house somewhere without the knowledge of her husband. The house was at a finishing level at the time of our discussion. She said her husband has no plan for the future of the children and the entire family. They have lived in a rented apartment for years. They struggle to feed, struggle to renew their rent. Childrens' school fees are none of his business. Hmmm! A genuine source of worry to any responsible spouse isn't' it?

I told her that the project will be a pleasant surprise to her husband at completion. But I was wrong. The intention was for them to move into the property after a divorce or the death of the man. Did I hear you exclaim, my goodness! I was able, however, to bottle up my own surprise so that the discussion could continue.

What could make the breadwinner of the house abdicate his entire responsibility to his spouse in such reckless abandonment when he is not disabled, jobless or retired. The women interpret this as gloominess. They see an imminent shipwreck. A voyage of disaster. So developing a plan 'B' would be the only safety net available.

As a result, spouses begin to keep:

Secret deeds of assignment

Land papers are processed in secret. Such documents are kept far away from the reach of the spouse. The in-laws' cruel attitudes to the wife after the demise of their brother does not help matters.

This is why the wife must keep something somewhere to fall back to.

Questionable names on property receipts become a common thing. Receipts bear names that are not known by the members of the family. Change of ownership is done in a hurry.

Questionable next of kin leading to falsification of bank documents. False court affidavits, frozen bank accounts, and so on, the list continues.

8. Infidelity Black Box

Merriam-Webster's dictionary defines infidelity as "unfaithfulness to a moral obligation." It refers to the act or fact of having a romantic or sexual relationship with someone other than one's husband, wife, or partner." The Latin word Fidelis means faithfulness.

Infidelity came from the word 'infidel' meaning unbeliever. Hence, it describes the activities of an unbeliever. No believer in his right mind will go after someone else's wife. You must be an infidel to do that.

Hard saying, you say? But when you look at what is happening among God's people today you'll realize that I wasn't even hard enough. Couples have abandoned their marital obligations. They start keeping secret and unhealthy relationships here and there. Some of the unmarried ones carry over such secrets to their new homes.

Whenever the devil decides to ruin a home; he makes the couple look down on themselves. They start seeing nothing but deficiencies. He makes them regret their present relationships, offering them solace outside their matrimonial arrangements.

In my twenty-seven years of counseling experience, eight out of every ten counselees on marital infidelity were women who had issues with their husbands. These women expressed different levels of emotional torture as a result of their husbands' secret affairs outside their matrimonial homes.

The truth is that men are more easily infatuated than women. That notwithstanding, heeding to the cautions in the book of Proverbs below will provide the man a lot of protection.

The Bible seems to beam its light on the man as seen below. Probably because of his assumed tendencies. No scripture can be as direct and explicit on marital faithfulness as Proverbs 5:15

Proverbs 5:15 "Be faithful to your own wife and give your love to her alone." (GNB)

This is a wife's exclusive domain. The husband's marital love is made for his wife and for the wife alone. Any other secret show of love is forbidden. *It is like a journey to the world of the dead. You're coming back is not guaranteed*. Yes as sweet as honey, but as deadly as a scorpion.

Proverbs 5:3-8 "The lips of another man's wife may be as sweet as honey and her kisses as smooth as olive oil, but when it is all over, she leaves you nothing but bitterness and pain. She will take you down to the world of the dead; the road she walks is the road to death...Keep away from such a woman! Don't even go near her door!" (GNB)

"Keep away from such a woman," the Bible warns, and 'Don't even go near her door" was the admonition. Nobody in his right mind takes a walk on a road that leads to death.

Proverbs 5:18 "So be happy with your wife and find your joy with the woman you married." (GNB)

Proverbs 5:19-20 "Let her be as the loving hind and pleasant roe; let her breasts satisfy thee at all times; and be thou ravished always with her love. And why wilt thou, my son, be ravished with a strange woman, and embrace the bosom of a stranger?"

The above scriptures have the remedy. You just have to be satisfied with your own wife, working together in prayer to address the undesirables. Your marriage is a project in God's hands. His Angels are at work to help you. This is possible if you believe.

Let Proverbs 5:21 be your watch Scripture.

Proverbs 5:21 "The LORD sees everything you do. Wherever you go, he is watching." (GNB)

Things For Which Couples Should Watch

1. The Danger of Aborted Love.

Couples should be careful not to keep a strong tie with their former girlfriends and former boyfriends, including those who had reasons whatsoever to remarry. Every covenant should be broken without necessary maintaining malice.

A wide gap is necessary even if the separation involved had pain, distrust, and unbearable emotional hurt. These might have healed over time as you learn to love and forgive people. The flesh should be tamed not to take undue advantage of this healing to long for its first love.

Be open. Tell your spouse about the child you had with Mr. 'A' before marriage. She will also need to know that the boy at home with mama is your child and not a relation deployed to assist mama with the domestics

The Bible says, when spouses keep secrets about their former relationships it is like one who covereth violence with his garment. The violence is not going to be there. It is there already waiting for the day the garment will be uncovered. Remember there is nothing hidden that shall not be revealed.

Malachi 2:16 "...for one covereth violence with his garment, saith the LORD of hosts: therefore take heed to your spirit, that ye deal not treacherously."

You Don't Have to be the Sixth Husband

Jesus told the Samaritan woman at the well in **John 4:16-18** "Go, call thy husband, and come hither. The woman answered and said, I have no husband. Jesus said unto her, Thou hast well said, I have no husband: For thou hast had five husbands; and he whom thou now hast is not thy husband: in that saidst thou truly."

Remember the woman first said she has no husband. She spoke like one of those urban girls in search of greener pastures. They behave as if they had never known any man in the flesh. They keep back all information about their lives that might discourage the next innocent suitor. This woman was like telling the Lord "young man I am available."

This is a caution statement. My brothers and sisters you don't have to be the sixth husband or wife. If you ask the Lord He will tell you which woman has had five husbands so that you don't become the sixth.

The days are evil the Scripture said. Very often, we see young men and women who were married elsewhere migrating to the cities where they pose as virgin bachelors and spinsters. They get involved in churches and before you know it, they are deeply hooked in another relationship.

In one such wedding, gunmen invaded the church, shooting in the air to stop the 'ungodly' solemnization. That was no terror attack. The priest fled and the congregation scattered. We got to know that the bridegroom has a wife and children at home. If we don't depend on God for guidance; you will find yourself hooked up with unsuitable people in life.

2. Complications of Unfaithfulness

• **Families are plunged into shame and ridicule**
(Taking Judah's family as a case study in **Genesis 38:6-26**)

The conception of Zerah and Pharez by their grandfather is a matrimonial disorder. For God's sake, how can you be the biological father of your grandchildren?

Genesis 38:15-16 "When Judah saw her, he thought her to be an harlot; because she had covered her face, And he turned unto her by the way, and said, Go to, I pray thee, let me come in unto thee; (for he knew not that she was his daughter in law.) And she said, What wilt thou give me, that thou mayest come in unto me?"

• **Diseases with unknown origin emerge**
• **The society is bastardized with children of unknown parents**

A man once refused to join the new church started by his wife. He also warned that none of his children will join her. Then the wife opened up and spilled the beans. " Mr. Man, for your information, you are not the biological father of these children," she said. In this world, the things we do not know seemed to be more than the ones we know. Jesus said it must be exposed one day.

• **God is provoked**
• **Vows are broken**
• **The Marriage Covenant is at stake**
• **The family comes under a curse.**

1 Corinthians 6:16 "What? Know ye not that he which is joined to an harlot is one body? For two, saith he, shall be one flesh."

When you sleep with anyone outside of marriage, you are in for a joint venture. You become a shareholder in the business. You share her demons, you share her curses, you share everything she has. The same with the man. It is not all over after the deal.

- **Trust is sacrificed on the altar of suspicion**
- **Separation and divorce are possible**
- **Children often bear the brunt**
- **Setback to the kingdom of God**
- **Satan is empowered to act**

3. Occult Membership

It is surprising or rather embarrassing that couples would belong to certain secret or occult groups unknown to their partners.

Some attend church services and still maintain their nominal role in various secret organizations. In some cases, the partner gets to know during the funeral. When strange and uninvited cult members arrive at the venue to claim certain funeral right from the bereaved family. I witnessed one of such funerals during which the cult members insisted on dissecting the body of the deceased. They said the heart belonged to them. And they must take it otherwise the body cannot be buried.

Some other cult groups may demand a huge

amount of money. In the midst of the fracas, they will threaten the death of the entire community should the bereaved family fail to pay up.

Because they usually appear in a strange regalia, the people panic and tremble. But what can be done? When even the officiating priestly would be asking for the settlement or he leaves. Hmmm! Dear couple all these happening just because of one secret action.

Nocturnal Movement of One Spouse with a Spiritualist.

I don't think it was in any of the National dailies, the night King Saul sneaked out to visit the witch at Endor. It was just one of the movements the big boys make without the consent of their wives. It is also very common with the politicians.

1 Samuel 28:3 & 7-8 "...And Saul had put away those that had familiar spirits, and the wizards, out of the land. Then said Saul unto his servants, Seek me a woman that hath a familiar spirit, that I may go to her, and enquire of her. And his servants said to him, Behold, there is a woman that hath a familiar spirit at Endor. And Saul disguised himself, and put on other raiment, and he went, and two men with him, and they came to the woman by night: and he said, I pray thee, divine unto me by the familiar spirit, and bring me him up, whom I shall name unto thee."

These days, the devil has rebranded it. He now calls it 'prayer houses'. Some of them operate only at nights and on hilltops. They market all manners of spiritual objects and material in the name of 'Spiritual Point of Contacts'. These are in turn brought home by the visiting spouse without the partner's knowledge. Those objects ultimately become a link and a window of attacks to the family.

These objects include the following:
- **Special Oil**
- **Holy Water**
- **Anointed Handkerchiefs**
- **Special Bangles, Anklets and Rings etc**
- **Special Candles, Incense, and Perfumes**
- **Holy Books.eg prayer books**
- **Good Luck Preparations**
- **Wonder Pens**
- **Ancestral Properties in the name of inheritance**
- **Spiritual Toys**
- **Love Potions**
- **Holy Emblems, Etc.**

4. god Traffickers

The question is, what are you bringing home? In the case of Rachel, in Genesis 31, she stole a household god. Did I hear you shout "stealing a god?" Yes, she did. In our days Rachel represents a wife of an Anointed man of God. A man who was carrying about a great nation called Israel. Of course, women are not left out in this secret behaviors.

Rachel's action was done without the consent of her husband Jacob. Rachel's life was on the line. The deal was to put to death anyone with his god. Unknown to Jacob, his wife had the god. During the search, she sat on it.

Genesis 31: 34-35 "Now Rachel had taken the images, and put them in the camel's furniture, and sat upon them. And Laban searched all the tent, but found them not."

She lied using a false menstrual condition as a weapon to further conceal her secret actions. This is common among women.

35 "And she said to her father, Let it not displease my lord that I cannot rise up before thee; for the custom of women is upon me. And he searched but found not the images."

Such a happy exodus back home after a long sojourn in the land of a wicked uncle could have been bastardized by the death of Rachel if the secret had been uncovered. She tightened the lead with a lie. Imagine what would have become of Jacob. A wife he got after fourteen years of hard labour.

The repercussions are innumerable.

The death of King Saul was not unconnected to his nocturnal visit to Endor. The Bible says:

1 Chronicles 10:13-14 "So Saul died for his transgression which he committed against the LORD, even against the word of the LORD, which he kept not, and also for asking counsel of one that had a familiar spirit, to enquire of it;

14 And enquired not of the LORD: therefore he slew him, and turned the kingdom unto David the son of Jesse."

King Solomon was a victim too. When you marry your partner with his or her gods: God will divorce you in a hurry. So don't permit god smugglers into your homes.

1 Kings 11:1 & 4 "But King Solomon loved many strange women, together with the daughter of Pharaoh, women of the Moabites, Ammonites, Edomites, Zidonians, and Hittites: For it came to pass, when Solomon was old, that his wives turned away his heart after other gods: and his heart was not perfect with the LORD his God, as was the heart of David his father."

So be careful to observe partners who show secret allegiance to traditionalists. They are festival fanatics. They observe all manners of festivals in the name of tradition. These people can import all manners of spiritual contraband into their homes without the knowledge of their partners. Running one's home with the tradition of men, instead of God's words is very dangerous.

5. Black Box of Concealed Health Issues

A lot of people don't believe in discussing their health condition with anybody, not even with their spouse. They share some information with their doctors, while concealing others for the fear of a bombshell diagnosis.

Suitors are also kept in the dark in order to keep the relationship. Unfortunately, those who used the cover-up methods are sometimes the first to experience a matrimonial crash. "Pastor, I was deceived into this relationship," is a common response we get from the aggrieved partner. "If he or she had told me, I could have prepared for it," they usually say.

Yes, it is natural for guys to become reluctant, especially when they hear unpleasant stories about their spouse. Most women also dislike digging backward. They believe the past should be allowed to remain in the past. But for God's sake, these are health issues. Your spouse should be the number one healthcare official in your life. They are the only one beside you when every other person has gone to sleep. So to suddenly surprise him with a concealed health challenge will not be a pleasant one.

We have had cases of:
- **Impotence**
- **Low Sperm Count**
- **No Sperm Condition**
- **No Womb Condition**
- **Artificial Breast Condition**
- **No Hair Condition**
- **Positive HIV Status**
- **Hepatitis**
- **Genotype**
- **And so on**

Thank God for the level of health awareness today. Other thanks to the various organizations that take their time to dig deep into these issues long before solemnization.

CHAPTER 11

THE CHALLENGE OF DELAYED PREGNANCY

I will always remember the night I knocked at the room belonging to one of my uncle's wives. I had been hearing the voice of one crying and wailing. I listened more attentively and behold, it was her voice. The cry went on for a very long time.

When I looked at the clock, it was about 2 am. What could a high school boy do? So many questions in my mind. The conclusion that she may have had a nightmare was not sufficient. Another thought that her life could be in danger drove me to her door.

I started asking her a number of questions which she did not answer. Still sobbing bitterly, she told me to go back to sleep, that I will not understand. When she saw I had joined the weeping, she decided to open up. What was it?

She had had a quarrel with one of the other wives during the day. This resulted in a hot exchange of words during which she was asked to prove if indeed she was a woman or a man in a female attire posing as a wife. Hmm! "A man in a female attire posing as a wife?" What on earth could that mean? We all know she is a woman I remembered what she said "… you will not understand." But how could that make a grown-up lady, a woman like her stay without food, weeping throughout the night? Oh! I still did not understand.

Friends, this is not a common tune to which everyone knows how to dance. It is a story that is better told by the afflicted. Eighteen years of marriage! God have mercy.

Hannah's situation was not any different. She had a Peninnah to contend with.

1 Samuel 1:4-7
"And when the time was that Elkanah offered, he gave to Peninnah his wife, and to all her sons and her daughters, portions:

5 But unto Hannah he gave a worthy portion; for he loved Hannah: but the LORD had shut up her womb.

6 And her adversary also provoked her sore, for to make her fret, because the LORD had shut up her womb.

7 And as he did so year by year, when she went up to the house of the LORD, so she provoked her; therefore she wept, and did not eat."

So Unworthy for A Worthy Portion

In verse 5, the Bible said, "But unto Hannah, he gave a worthy portion; for he loved Hannah: but the LORD had shut up her womb."

Worthy portions? Yes; so much love? Yes. However, no woman accepts that as compensation for a shut womb. The issue of the husband being better to a woman than ten sons does not arise in the first place. Women can only accept their husbands as ceremonial sons, not in reality. This is common in Africa.

No doubt, husbands are regarded as the old boys of the house. They are the sweetest babies at home, the firstborn of the woman, but never a son to a childless woman. Otherwise, those women with Elkanah as husbands will cease to worry about delayed pregnancy.

Hannah was lucky. The majority of the women in her condition don't usually have an assuring husband like Elkanah The reason is not far-fetched.

In most cultures, the pressure on the husband is also unbearable. The man sees himself as worthless and voiceless fellow amidst his kinsmen. Some relatives could be blunt with him, especially under the influence of alcohol. Publicly, they will ask him why he married a fellow man instead of a woman? And because he has no hope of an heir apparent; he would not be man enough to talk in the community. He becomes a laughingstock in the clan.

So, many traditional restrictions are placed on him. Mockers will accuse him of having used his manhood for money rituals. As a result, the husband comes home and turns all the heat on the wife.

No one will blame Rachel who in her situation puts it this way to Jacob: "…Give me children or else I die" **Genesis 30:1**.

Friend, this was neither a threat nor emotional blackmail to the Patriarch, Jacob. But an outburst from the heart of a desperate woman.

When the children begin to arrive, the problem changes from 'no child' to 'no son.' And unfortunately, it is believed that women are the cause of it all. She is either a witch or a sponsored agent from the Marine world. This is common in most African countries.

The church is not spared. Some so-called repentant folks ignorantly vowed never to let go of such satanic ideology.

I know of a fellow minister who drove away his wife and children and married another woman.

What was her offense? Was she childless? No. Was she caught in adultery? No. Then what? Well, just because she has no male child. The man did not hide his concern. "Who will take over from me when I am gone" he will argue with anyone who challenges him.

The question is, "Has the church become a traditional institution?" God forbid. This was Jesus' answer when His disciples were confronted by a traditional-religious sect over certain violations.

Mark 7:9 "Then He told them, "You have such a fine way of rejecting the commandment of God in order to keep your tradition" (ISV).

The church should not allow this ugly trend, no matter what their fine reasons may be. Unlike your tradition, Jesus never taught His disciples to divorce the wife without a male child.

The parents of the couple are not helping matters themselves. They are more interested in their grandchildren than in the grand trauma the condition has generated. Hmm! The ordeal of a childless mother. The above scenario is nothing compared to what a number of these couples in certain quarters go through.

I would like you to know that you are not alone in this situation. God knows how you feel. You did not stumble across this book by accident. It is an indication that God has picked up your case file.

Thank God for civilized societies and cultures where you have less of these problems. They have access to advanced medical facilities. An adoption is also a common option in such a society. This is not the same elsewhere. It is hellish for the rest of the world. We know it is still a struggle for some believers. However you may feel, God is not yet done with your situation. He knows all about your struggles, according to the songwriter. And has come to wipe away your tears.

God Has Remembered You

Yes! He has! No doubt about it. This is not to say He forgot you in the first place. God does not suffer dementia.

His cognitive ability does not deteriorate as in the case of one with Alzheimer's disease. He is All-Knowing. He remembers what happened the first day man was placed on this planet. He can also choose to forget what happened the last second. He forgets what He wants to forget and remembers them no more. He did just that to our ugly past. This is why He is God. Here is what prophet Isaiah said:

Isaiah 43:25 "I, I am the one who blots out your transgression for my own sake, and I'll remember your sins no more." (ISV)

Your Condition Is Not A Sentence

Child of God, don't agree with the devil - the accuser of the brethren- that your condition was a sentence for your ugly past. God does not work with your past. That's why He blotted out your past. To 'blot' means to remove. And according to Merriam Webster's Dictionary, it means: "To dry with absorbing agents." Jesus was the Absorbing Agent.

The Apostle Paul puts it this way: **Colossians 2:14** "Blotting out the handwriting of ordinances that was against us, which was contrary to us, and took it out of the way, nailing it to his cross."

Friends, the above scripture is worth your celebration. The moment you surrender your life to the Lord Jesus; you become a new creation. You may not look it, but that's what you are. This includes your reproductive organs.

See how Apostle Paul puts it: **2 Corinthians 5:17** "Therefore if any man be in Christ, he is a new creature: old things are passed away; behold, all things are become new."

Beloved, this newness position is necessary for your miracle to happen. These include a new womb, a new uterus, new fallopian tubes, new sperm cells and so on.

Yes, the devil will tell you that you are not the kind of person pastor is talking about. He will tell you that your case is beyond remedy. He will remind you that the abortion was not just once as was the case of your friend who later took in after many years of waiting. He will convince you to accept that you are too dirty to receive anything from this holy God. Don't you ever believe him?

Some Testimonies That Will Boost Your Faith

I appeal to the recipients of these great miracles that I am about to share, to join me in prayer so that God will use it to encourage the readers who may be passing through similar life challenges. I will try not to divulge your identity should you not be comfortable making the testimonies public.

At the beginning of this chapter, I shared with you the pathetic story of my uncle's wife. Today she has five grown-up children. She lives in the village and has no access to advanced medical care.

In her case, God alone did it. There are times He

would use the hands of the physicians. God fulfilled all the Scriptures I used to share with her during her wilderness experience. What a wonderful God! Thank you, Jesus.

I went to the bank for a normal banking transaction. A lady that looked like one of the senior bank officials walked straight up to me. She said someone in her told her to go and share her problem with me. Just like that? I was not wearing anything that identified me as a pastor.

In my mind, I felt that was a very dangerous step anyone can take. She may be heading to pour her heart to an evil man. I asked her if she knew who I was? She replied, "Not at all, but that the Spirit of God ministered to her to meet me and share the problem with me."

I noticed that the moment I asked her what the problem was, the power of God came upon me right there. The spiritual atmosphere was set for a miracle. I knew that God was about to give her a solution.

She said she'd been married for years, but instead of children, miscarriages were the order of the day. All her medical efforts did not yield the expected result. Right under that unction, I held her hands and decreed an end to that awful experience. And God honoured our prayers. She has weaned her second child now. Who can battle with the Lord?

May I Pray For You

If your case is that of frequent miscarriages, I would like you to place your hands on your stomach if you don't mind and say this prayer after me.

In the Name of Jesus, I bring my Spirit, my Soul and my Body under the influence of the Holy Spirit. I take my position of sonship in the Lord and therefore make the following decrees and declarations:

- My womb hear thou the words of the Lord. "There shall nothing cast their young, nor be barren, in thy land: the number of thy days I will fulfill." **Exodus 23:26**
- In the Name of Jesus, I cleanse you from any impediment. From today on you will be conducive to do your nine-month assignment. You will no more cast my seeds young.
- You did it before, but now the word of God forbids a repeat of such unholy circle. This is what the Lord said "What do ye imagine against the LORD? he will make an utter end: affliction shall not rise up the second time." **Nahum 1:9**
- Lord, I place Your Words above the activities of witches, bloodsucking spirits, and ancestral manipulations. I declare myself a fruitful vine according to Your Word. "Thy wife shall be as a fruitful vine by the sides of thine house: thy children like olive plants round about thy table." **Psalms 128:3.**

- Thank you, Lord, because I shall have my baby this time around in Jesus name, Amen! And Amen!!

More Testimonials

Friends, if a woman without a womb can conceive and give birth to a child, distorting medical literature; you that still have your wombs intact have a much less complicated matter to trust God for. This happened in our ministry in Zaria, Kaduna state of Nigeria. According to my Papa, the womb was removed intentionally with the couples consent for health reasons. This indeed was an all-time miracle and a display of the omnipotent power of our God.

Beloved, your case may not be as bad as the above condition. God has the human spare parts in His storehouse. That is why He has no regard for any womb or sperm situation. God has never met a complicated matter. Issues are only complicated with men.

I was ministering the Word during a worship service and it was heavily laid in my heart to call those who were trusting God for the fruit of the womb. Amongst those who came for prayer was this beloved sister who joined us from another ministry.

I called her aside after the service for a few minute counseling session. Because of her age, I wanted to know if she was standing in for someone else or came for prayer for herself. She said it was for herself. I became a little bit cautious at this time and my counsel was in favour of adoption. She said "Pastor your job is to pray and you have done that excellently well. The rest is not your job." Hmmm! What a great woman of faith. What else will I say—then may it be done accordingly to your faith. To shorten the testimony, we dedicated her twin babies on one of the Sundays. That is your God. He is no respecter of persons.

I went with some people to the Israeli embassy for an appointment. While we were waiting for our turn, a lady sitting next to me pleaded if I could spare five minutes of my time to listen to her. I replied, "Why not?"

I presumed her topic to be about trending national issues in order to while away our waiting time. But I was wrong.

First, she introduced herself as Barrister 'X'. And I replied, I am Agala. I did not include the word pastor. Right there she told me her story. She said her husband had commenced an arrangement to bring home his secretary as his new wife. She said this would be finalized in three months time. I wanted to know what she did to her husband. She said her offense was she was childless. Already in tears, she said she did not know why she must tell me her story.

Well, I tried to control myself at this point. I was more interested in what God would want me to do in the infectious weeping. I wondered why God would prefer to assign His cases to mortal men, instead of handling them directly by Himself when identified.

As we began to pray, the word of God came. I told

her that the three-month duration has been converted as her first trimester. We also asked God to shatter and torpedo that strange marriage agenda. She collected my phone number and promised to call me. Her burden was literary lifted and she went home rejoicing.

Her call came after nine long months. She had misplaced my phone number. She said that God answered our prayer just the way we asked Him. God shattered the husband's relationship with the secretary and she became pregnant the very month of our meeting. She miraculously found my number before the child's dedication. She said I must, by all means, be there for the dedication. But, unfortunately, I was on my way to the airport traveling to the US. Friends, Jesus is the same yesterday, today and forever.

My experience in America was one of the most humbling experiences I have ever had. A very beloved servant of God asked me to preach in his church.

At the end of the service, a young man who was the head usher and his wife approached me and said that God told them to lodge me in their house and their fourteen-year-old prayer request will be granted. A fourteen-year-old prayer request?

Anyway, still thinking what a fourteen-year-old prayer request could be; I told them I cannot decide on that all alone. It is against ministerial ethics. I have never been to that church before. I had no relationships with members. It wouldn't be proper for me to leave my hotel room for the house of a member without the consent of the pastor.

When the man of God discovered that another brother was also interested in hosting me; he asked me to consent to their request as well saying that that could be God going to their houses. What a wonderful congregation! At this point, a temporary schedule was drawn and the first brother chose to be the last host.

I checked out of the hotel. Following the schedule, the second brother took me to his house. We had great fellowship together and at the end of his scheduled time, the head usher took me to his house, marking the beginning of another great miracle.

They told me how they had waited for the past fourteen years for a child. They were actually planning to bring a man of God from Africa. This man of God had told them that if they could bring him to America to stay with them for one week, then they would have their baby. He said the moment he saw me coming into the church, God told him that this was the man you should bring to your house. God confirmed the same message with his wife.

I told them that God did not tell me that. And again, I don't have babies to distribute to people. I don't know how the African pastor planned to go about doing this on his own. One thing I know was that if it is God who told you, He will surely bring it to pass.

We went into series of prayers and waiting upon the Lord. We were just doing things we were led to do. A room was dedicated for the unborn child with all manners of baby stuff. Needless to say, all the things we did prophetically. The summary was that the baby came and was delivered the fifteenth year.

I don't know how long you have waited. During the last two Sundays, we dedicated twin babies that came out of a twenty-three-year barren womb. No need telling you the age of the mother. For your information, if Mama Sarah's womb can carry a baby at the age of 90, then your womb is not too young for a similar assignment. Thinking God has forgotten your condition is a vindictive lie from the enemy.

As children's pastor, she continued to serve the Lord faithfully in that capacity until the day of her visitation. The church prayed all manner of prayers and took so many prophetic steps on her behalf. I was not left out. The last time we met, I told her I was going to sew the garment I would wear on the day of her baby dedication. Which dedication? But that was my own prophetic action. As I was wearing the garment two Sundays ago for the dedication, I saw a God who is faithful and unfailing in His love.

For anyone suffering from erectile dysfunction, low or no sperm count, life is not yet over for you. What you need is a miracle and God can give you that miracle now. A testimony will emerge out of your frustrations in Jesus name. Hear what God did for others.

My pastor friend invited me to come and dedicate his baby the second week of August this year. He had come down with diabetes and high blood pressure. He was hospitalized and in a coma for weeks. It was a long battle for over a year. At the end when they wanted to start having babies, the man had lost his erections.

They went back to the hospital and the doctors told them that this was a condition they just have to accept as a complication of diabetes. There were other things the doctors did not tell them, such thing as his having no sperm count.

This couple cried and later accepted their condition, as it were. At least, that the husband came back to life was a consolation.

All of a sudden, the wife set aside the medical reports and went back to God in prayer. During the prayer period, she became sick and had to go to the hospital. She was having strange feelings in her belly. But guess what? She had become pregnant. Did I hear you shout 'pregnant! How? Well, God knows how. For God, that frustrated sex they had that day was enough. In the Name of Jesus, I see your frustrations turning into a miracle.

The husband threw away the pregnancy test result sheet. She must explain to him who was responsible. Another big issue erupted. Oh, satan must be a bad devil. I remembered when I was invited to settle a couple whose wife said she was pregnant by the spirit when her husband traveled. Of course, that ended the marriage as her husband vowed never to allow another virgin birth in his house other than the one that was prophesied. But this was a raw miracle from God and the devil wanted to use it to separate the family? God forbid. Thank God who intervened when it was confirmed that it was his child.

I was in Ghana to perform a wedding for a minister friend. I went to see a relative after the wedding. A young man who was going home after the Sunday service stopped to say hi to my friend. On his way out, he turned back and told my brother that God clearly told him to go back and ask the man in his house to pray for him. He came and knelt down before me and said: "Sir I am a pastor with… I got married many years ago and up till now, we have no child" This happened without anyone revealing my identity to him.

However, I felt so unworthy and unable to fathom why God was doing this. Well, I make sure I refer the people back to Him. It is not about me. I am neither a spiritual gynecologist nor a kingdom infertility expert. I have only shared with you an eyewitness account of what your God can do. God shows no partiality or favoritism in dealing with people.

The Apostle Paul put it this way: **Acts 10:34-35** "Then Peter opened his mouth, and said, Of a truth, I perceive that God is no respecter of persons: But in every nation he that feareth him, and worketh righteousness, is accepted with him."

Child of God, can't you see that God is already at work in your case? It is indeed not too late for you to testify. What He did for one: He can do for another.

Other Selected Scriptures To Build Your Faith
Isaiah 54:4
"Don't be afraid, because you won't be ashamed; don't fear shame, for you won't be humiliated—

because you will forget the disgrace of your youth, and the reproach of your widowhood you will remember no more." (ISV)

Deuteronomy 7:14

"Thou shalt be blessed above all people: there shall not be male or female barren among you, or among your cattle."

This covers the both of you. "…there shall not be male or female barren among you."

Judges 13:2-3

"And there was a certain man of Zorah, of the family of the Danites, whose name was Manoah; and his wife was barren, and bare not. And the angel of the LORD appeared unto the woman, and said unto her, Behold now, thou art barren, and bearest not: but thou shalt conceive, and bear a son."

1 Samuel 2:5

"They that were full have hired out themselves for bread; and they that were hungry ceased: so that the barren hath born seven; and she that hath many children is waxed feeble."

Psalm 113:9

"He maketh the barren woman to keep house, and to be a joyful mother of children. Praise ye the LORD."

Isaiah 54:1

"Sing, O barren, thou that didst not bear; break forth into singing, and cry aloud, thou that didst not travail with child: for more are the children of the desolate than the children of the married wife, saith the LORD."

Luke 1:36

"And, behold, thy cousin Elisabeth, she hath also conceived a son in her old age: and this is the sixth month with her, who was called barren."

Luke 23:29

"For, behold, the days are coming, in the which they shall say, Blessed are the barren, and the wombs that never bare, and the paps which never gave suck."

Galatians 4:27

"For it is written, Rejoice, thou barren that bearest not; break forth and cry, thou that travailest not: for the desolate hath many more children than she which hath an husband."

Prayers Don't Expire: So Don't Give Up

Child of God, something begins to happen when you begin to pray. It doesn't matter how long you have prayed. God does not ignore people when they pray. One would, therefore, be insulting God when they make such statements as: "I prayed and nothing happened."

The Prophet Isaiah puts it this way: **Isaiah 65:24** "And it shall come to pass, that before they call, I will answer; and while they are yet speaking, I will hear."

1 John 5:14 "And this is the confidence that we have in him, that, if we ask anything according to his will, he heareth us."

Yes, He heareth us. So do not delete that seemingly 'unanswered' prayer point from your list just because something has not happened in the physical. You have prayed for the past twenty years. Keep praying. The rule is: pray until you take the delivery. The Angels are at work for your sake. Something is going on that you do not know. It happened to Daniel.

Danel 10:12 "Then said he unto me, Fear not, Daniel: for from the first day that thou didst set thine heart to understand, and to chasten thyself before thy God, thy words were heard, and I am come for thy words."

A prayer of twenty-one days was heard on the first day. Come on, God is not deaf. Yes, He's not. But don't stop.

This is different from what the Lord condemned in **Matthew 6:7**

"But when ye pray, use not vain repetitions, as the heathen do: for they think that they shall be heard for their much speaking."

God will never describe the prayers of His children as vain repetition. You are not the heathen who pray just to show the people that they are praying. Your prayers could move from asking to thanking. In any case, don't stop until you take the delivery.

Luke 1:7;13-14 "And they had no child, because that Elisabeth was barren, and they both were now well stricken in years. But the angel said unto him, Fear not, Zacharias: for thy prayer is heard; and thy wife Elisabeth shall bear thee a son, and thou shalt call his name John. And thou shalt have joy and gladness, and many shall rejoice at his birth."

Couples are often blessed at weddings the same way God commanded them to be fruitful in the garden. They go home to continue with the prayer. Couples, however, receive their answers at different times and seasons. Mother Elisabeth got hers when she was well stricken in age. Mary was visited even before her wedding by Divine Choice.

These people had one thing in common. They were busy and actively serving the Lord in their waiting. Zechariah was on duty when God visited him. The Angel told him his prayers had been answered. Which prayers? Of course, the prayer for the fruit of the womb which may have ranked topmost in their prayer list when they got married. But time has deleted that. Hmm! More questions than answers. To them, such a request was no longer relevant. It had expired.

You know the end of the story. God struck him dumb to avoid further discussion on the matter. Friends, prayer does not expire until the problems expire. Tell the analyst to reserve their comments till the day you will be naming and dedicating your baby. I can't wait for your testimonies.

CHAPTER 12

ASUNDER IS NOT FROM YONDER

"We've been told for decades now that half of all marriages end in divorce – and that it's only getting worse." The ***Refinery 29*** publications traced this position back to a 1980 census report. The report predicted that "half of the couples married between 1976 and 1977 would eventually end up divorced and that rates would only increase from there." The publishers explained that "researchers have found that the rate of divorce in the U.S. actually peaked at about 40% around 1980 and has been declining ever since." **www.refinery29.com/2017/01/13744**

That's good news, isn't it? But before we celebrate the decline, there is something more worrisome in their research finding. Amongst the listed factors that can affect divorce rate was 'Religion.' Others were Age, Education Level, Location, Race, Sexuality, Children, etc.

Here are their findings on Religion. "In general, having a stronger connection to religion tends to keep a marriage more stable. But that certainly doesn't mean religious people don't get divorced. A Pew analysis found that, among those who have divorced, 74% were Christian and 20% were agnostic or atheists."

According to the online publication, **www.divorce-online.co.uk;** the latest divorce statistics for the UK also shows a downward trend. This is the same for new marriages. According to them, the fall in the number of marriages to 2009 is more likely due to the increasing number of couples choosing to cohabit rather than get married.

To 'cohabit' means, "to live together and have a sexual relationship." It also means "to live together as or as if a married couple." (Merriam Webster Dictionaries) Hmmm! This looks like a panacea to this generational monster called divorce. The logic is straightforward. If we are not legally married, we have nothing to do with divorce.

I tried to imagine for a second, a world where men merely cohabit with women. The picture I got was that of the animal kingdom and the world as a jungle, in which the hallowed institution of marriage is reduced to mere human cohabitation. An association of sex partners in which no one is matrimonially responsible. I consider this a dangerous downward trend. It means we are yet to arrive at what we can comfortably call a way out.

Friends, the purpose of this chapter is not to bug anyone with divorce statistics. The trend could be upward or downward as the case may be. God is not after the trends, but the stoppage.

Here is What He said in His Word:

Malachi 2:16 "I hate divorce," says the Lord God of Israel, "the one who is guilty of violence," says the Lord who rules over all. "Pay attention to your conscience, and do not be unfaithful." **(NET)**.

I know I am on a head-on collision with some legal provisions enshrined in most Federal and State laws. Some of our laws are escapee provisions designed to make the injured stop crying while the injury is left untreated. This is human articulation in principle.

God says He hates divorce, period. You don't need further legislation where God already has His verdict. **"...says the Lord who rules over all."** Here God declared Himself as the Attorney General of the Universe.

The church must arise and with one voice condemn this 'family disorder' called divorce. Stop searching for scriptures with which to counter what God said. The lawyers have made fortunes from our disobedience. It is high time we deleted divorce cases from their schedules.

Yes, many countries of the world have revolted against God their maker by legalizing those things

God said He hates. The church mustn't join them. No wonder the world is yet to see rebellion. The parliaments are busy working against God in their legislation. What a generation.

Child of God, this is a covenant of infusion. One flesh is not separable. That is why he said:

Genesis 2:24 "Therefore shall a man leave his father and his mother, and shall cleave unto his wife: and they shall be one flesh."

I know I am gradually losing your friendship by now. You are thinking your case is the worse scenario ever. And it has never happened to anyone before. That is a lie from the devil. Here Is what Apostle Paul said in his letter to the Corinthians:

1 Corinthians 10:13 "There hath no temptation taken you but such as is common to man: but God is faithful, who will not suffer you to be tempted above that ye are able; but will with the temptation also make a way to escape, that ye may be able to bear it."

There is no family problem that cannot be resolved in God. Did you see such phrases as: ."..**but God is faithful,..**" and "**...way to escape,**" in the above scriptures? I don't think '**divorce**' is one of those escape routes He had in mind. Also, note that it is not the judge or jury that made this promise. It is God. So run to God and not to court especially where the parties involved are followers of Christ.

Yes, the judiciary is said to be the hope for the common man. There is no doubt about that. If not for the judiciary evil will triumph with impunity. Their adjudication is very important especially on criminal matters.

For a child of God, divorce is an exclusive case. God already has His verdict before the hearing. "**...I hate divorce," says the Lord God of Israel,..**" The court of God is willing to entertain all the cases that lead to divorce 'pro bono' (without pay)

God Has A Court: The Church

The church as constituted by God ought to function as the home for Alternative Dispute Resolution (ADR Centre). It is never intended to take over the judicial responsibilities. God gave the church the authority to adjudicate over any kind of dispute arising from the brethren. Here is Apostle Paul's position on this matter:

1 Corinthians 6: 1-7 "When any of you has a legal dispute with another, does he dare go to court before the unrighteous rather than before the saints? .." And if the world is to be judged by you, are you not competent to settle trivial suits?" (NET)

Disappointed over the ease at which brethren file up lawsuits against each other, the Apostle said in verse five:

"I say this to your shame! Is there no one among you wise enough to settle disputes between fellow Christians?" "...The fact that you have lawsuits among yourselves demonstrates that you have already been defeated." (NET)

The church is designed and empowered to settle both spiritual and most civil matters, using the lay down Biblical injections.

Every Bible believing child of God should know that the above scripture is an indictment against the church. More court congestion is caused by religious folks rather than robbers and murderers. The church should rise to her responsibility.

Some of you would like me to tread cautiously and gently with the subject matter arguing that divorce cases have so many legal implications and as such should be handled by a court of competent jurisdiction. You are right. But God wants the church to stop the divorce before it occurs. All that God was looking for was men '**wise enough**' to settle disputes between fellow Christians. They don't have to be legal luminaries. What is required is the wisdom of God.

"Is there no one among you wise enough to settle disputes between fellow Christians?"

The answer to the above question will awaken the church and their leadership to the God-given responsibility.

Marriage Vow: Not Divorce Vow

A lot of us had at different times recited the marriage vows. I don't know what pledges you made during your wedding. It is called 'exchange of marriage vows'. "...**Until death do us part**" must be among the things you promised that day.

You even declared publicly before God's holy congregation that "...**this is forever.**" It is treacherous to all of a sudden negate those marriage vows for whatever may be your good reason.

Some years back, at the end of a wedding service, the couple went home leaving behind their wedding gifts. I volunteered to convey the wedding gifts to their residence. I took some brethren along to help me take the gifts upstairs. I then noticed that the wrapped gifts were being thrown down out of the upstairs windows. Yes, they were the gifts the brethren were taking up. I thought perhaps we had the wrong address. I wished it was the case.

What on earth could have led to that type of sharp disagreement few hours after the marriage vows were made? They will have their reasons, won't they? I'm sure you are curious to know the end result. Well, the marriage ended the very day it started. That may have been the shortest marriage you have ever heard of. God have mercy.

Every day relationships are dismantled with reckless abandon. Church folks are not left behind. Even the leaders have become divorce champions. We are not living in the first dispensation. God has changed things. We need a reawakening. Stop looking for scriptures with which to disobey scriptures.

No Scripture Is A Divorce License

The scriptures below are not a license for divorce. There is no contradiction in God's Word. He does not have a double standard. He has the supreme authority to either ignore or permit. No mortal can charge Him with irregularity. There were certain things He permitted at a certain time in history when men were struggling to know Him. Don't make yourself a victim of primordial antecedence by marrying your own sister and support yourself with Father Abraham's example, or start targeting seven hundred wives and look the direction of King Solomon.

Deuteronomy 24:1-4 "When a man hath taken a wife, and married her, and it come to pass that she find no favour in his eyes, because he hath found some uncleanness in her: then let him write her a bill of divorcement, and give it in her hand, and send her out of his house. And when she is departed out of his house, she may go and be another man's wife. And if the latter husband hate her, and write her a bill of divorcement, and giveth it in her hand, and sendeth her out of his house..."

The above scripture is a "divorce made easy" isn't it? Just "Dislike her and Divorce her" Can't you see how chaotic things would have become. In fact, that may be the end of all marriages. Disastrous you say. Yes, because some folks would have finished divorcing their wives before reading this chapter.

The Lord Jesus did not deny the existence of such scriptures when He said: "It hath been said, Whosoever shall put away his wife, let him give her a writing of divorcement: But I say unto you..." Note that Jesus was not an editor. He is rather the Author. He knew what He said before and what He is saying now. He is the author and the finisher.

Matthew 5:31-34A "It hath been said, Whosoever shall put away his wife, let him give her a writing of divorcement: But I say unto you, That whosoever shall put away his wife, saving for the cause of fornication, causeth her to commit adultery: and whosoever shall marry her that is divorced committeth adultery. Again, ye have heard that it hath been said by them of old time, Thou shalt not forswear thyself, but shalt perform unto the Lord thine oaths: But I say unto you, Swear not at all..."

So we should drop our parochial arguments when He is talking.

The new teaching on divorce spread like a wildfire and caught the attention of the Pharisees. "The Pharisees also came..." meaning that many other religious groups had been coming in order to clarify this new teaching on divorce.

Matthew 19:3-10 "The Pharisees also came unto him, tempting him, and saying unto him, Is it lawful for a man to put away his wife for every cause? And he answered and said unto them, Have ye not read, that he which made them at the beginning made them male and female, And said, For this cause shall a man leave father and mother, and shall cleave to his wife: and they twain shall be one flesh? Wherefore they are no more twain, but one flesh. What therefore God hath joined together, let not man put asunder."

The Pharisees in verse seven were concerned if the rules had been changed when they cited Moses' commandment in this question below.

"They say unto him, Why did Moses then command to give a writing of divorcement, and to put her away? He saith unto them, Moses because of the hardness of your hearts suffered you to put away your wives: but from the beginning, it was not so." Jesus was frank and straightforward in His answer to the Pharisees. "...because of the hardness of your hearts."

This was not like a new agenda. It is just that people tend to flow with the convenience rather than with the context. Ramesh Richard, confirms this in his book '**Scripture Sculpture**' when he said: "Really the Bible can be made to say almost anything you may want it to say. The critical question is this. Are you saying what the Bible wanted to say?"

Jesus was simply restoring the marriage relationship to its original state. Referring to what the father has in mind from the beginning. So the permissive provision due to the hardness of their hearts should not be used against the original intention by moralists now and then.

Jesus Was Tough

The Lord was blunt in verse nine. The choice of the word '**whosoever**' was a direct shot to their personality. No exemption. I am a high priest or 'low' priest does not apply. Here is the way He puts it :

Matthew 19:9 "And I say unto you, Whosoever shall put away his wife, except it be for fornication, and shall marry another, committeth adultery: and whoso marrieth her which is put away doth commit adultery."

The above statement of Jesus seemed to put everyone on the spot; knowing fully well that the law has death as the penalty for adultery in:

Leviticus 20:10 "And the man that committeth adultery with another man's wife, even he that committeth adultery with his neighbour's wife, the adulterer and the adulteress shall surely be put to death."

This was a great concern to the people and enough to worry about.

The disciples had no hiding place either as there was no special provision or clause of exemption made for them as His followers. For them, the man is put at a disadvantage. Hence their conclusion as presented below.

"…His disciples say unto him, If the case of the man be so with his wife, it is not good to marry." But, still, Jesus did not promise an amendment. Rather He said in verse twelve: "…He that is able to receive it, let him receive it."

The Apostle Paul further quoted the Lord in:

1 Corinthians 7:10-11 "And unto the married I command, yet not I, but the Lord, Let not the wife depart from her husband: 11 But and if she depart, let her remain unmarried or be reconciled to her husband: and let not the husband put away his wife."

In **1 Corinthians 7:27** he concluded by saying: "Art thou bound unto a wife? seek not to be loosed. Art thou loosed from a wife? seek not a wife." This, I believe should supersede the old injunction of Deuteronomy Chapter Twenty four from verse one to four, where divorce was permitted due to the hardness of their hearts.

The promise of the Father in **Ezekiel 36:26** saying: "A new heart also will I give you, and a new spirit will I put within you: and I will take away the stony heart out of your flesh, and I will give you a heart of flesh", was totally fulfilled in the Lord through the principle of regeneration in the New Testament. It is indeed a good news to know that in our time the Lord offers a solution to the stony heart syndrome that plagued God's people during the time of Moses.

Praise God for the ease of obedience His Spirit through grace has offered us in the Gospel. Now we have hearts of flesh, sensitive to the commandments of the Lord and no more the former stone-hard hearts that are insensitive, stubborn and stiff-necked to the laws of God.

According to **The International Bible Commentary**, Edited by F. F. Bruce (1986) it was upheld that:

"Jesus comment on this Deuteronomic injunction, however, was that it did not represent God's absolute will, but something rather which, on account of the perversity of human heart, He permitted in order that the consequences of that perversity might be kept in restraint"

Brethren, Asunder is not from yonder. It is rather a process orchestrated by failure mechanism in human relationships. "...but from the beginning, it was not so" say the Lord.

Beloved couples, can I speak to your spirit. With this book in your hands, God is offering you a stage one solution to that complex situation. Stage two is your willingness to do the will of God. That your situation is one of its kind and has never happened to anyone before is a lie of the devil. Hear me, child of God, even if it is; God has a peculiar solution meant only for your peculiar situation.

The saying that "the Judiciary remains the hope for the common man" is not eliminated. The judiciary has done so well in checking the excesses of men. They can be very helpful where your partner is not a believer and does not submit to the laws of God. Here, the state laws should meet his or her need. This is necessary, more especially where the life of a partner is in danger.

"Pastor, I have tried everything that didn't work," you say. No doubt about that. However, obedience to an inspirational instruction may be all you need now. Things can change for you now. God is offering you last minute help. There is the possibility that those things you did in time past do not include what God wants you to do. In fact, both of you can start by believing God's Word.

If both of you are believers who love God, and your marriage is under attack, and you are already on your way to the court to start the divorce process, pick up your phone and cancel the appointment. Turn back to the Lord, the only Advocate the Judge of the whole world listens to. He knows what is causing the problem, unlike your lawyer. He will give you the judgment that will fill your heart with peace for the rest of your life.

Remember, there is no marriage that cannot come under attack in one form or another. Don't be in hurry to seek a replacement spouse. That man or woman out there is good enough just for their own wife or husband. Don't believe the comfort story of another man's bed. One night on such bed may give you a lifetime nightmare.

Rather, make your bed as comfortable as you would want it.

The ladies who wished their husbands were like me, were highly disappointed. I could see it all over their faces. Why? Because I told them that none of them can marry me for more than twenty hours without divorcing me in a hurry. But by the time I explained why, there was noise and the session became rowdy. Many said truly no woman can marry a man like that. Some hardliners amongst them said the twenty-four hours was even too long for them. The ushers finally achieved a decorum and there was silence again.

The silence did not last long. It erupted into clapping and shouting when I told them that my wife had been on it for the past twenty-five Years and still have no future plans of leaving my house.

This was not meant to be a run down on my integrity quotient. Just that I didn't realize at the time that most women tend to have zero tolerance for men who have "food problems." Regrettably, I happen to be one such man.

My eating problems started right from my childhood days. It was never a marriage-induced problem. It was rather marriage managed.

My mother will prepare a particular meal at my request. The moment the food was served, my appetite for the food will disappear for another kind of food. There is no guarantee that the third meal will make It to my stomach.

One of such days, she cried out to God in prayer. She asked God to please give me a wife that will tolerate that. I felt such prayer was grossly unnecessary. What has a wife to do with my food. I never knew wives have everything to do with food. I was not looking like someone who would ever get married. The only people I know that prepared meals were mothers. It never occurred to me then that these mothers are the same wives referred to. Well, the testimony is that God answered her prayers in my wife.

Sure, you now understand why your wife or husband is that special envoy from God to meet that peculiar needs of yours. Help-meet, the very help you require.

It is not an allegation that the devil is the sponsor of every divorce. He hates you and would want your home to join the list of the homes he has destroyed. Don't be gentle about it. He is mean and does not welcome dialogue. Bind him in prayer and take back your marriage by force.

Ask the Lord what your next steps should be. Take those steps and you will be amazed at the miracles.

Make these decrees and declarations with me in faith:

I see the Lord at work in my family.

I bind you, thou old serpent, who is working subtly behind the scene against my marriage. I sever every link you have with my family now in Jesus' Name.

I restore the joy of this family. I restore the peace of this family. I restore the love and unity of this family in the Mighty Name of the Lord Jesus.

From today on, no more fighting, no more quarreling, no more nagging in Jesus' name.

Thank you, Lord, for a total restoration of our marriage in Jesus' Name we pray, Amen.

REFERENCES FOR
THE FAMILY CLINIC

Stanley, Linda. www.whatscookingamerica.net ©2004-2015.

Neufeld, Joy M, and Wachsmann, Carrie. (1996) *The Healthiest People On Earth Cookbook* HeartBeat Productions Inc., 1996

Lindberg, Judy, and McFarland, Laura Gladys. *Aging Without Growing Old*, Siloam Press, 2003

USA Centre For Disease Control & Prevention Journal, www.cdc.gov/foodborneburden/index.htm.

Premium Times Web publication: Agency Report, Wednesday, March 1, 2017.
www.premiumtimesng.com>news

Elliott, Charlotte in her song 'Christian seek not yet repose' 1836

International Bible Society, *The Complete Christian Dictionary For Home And School*, 1992

Taniya Prusty's online publication, 1.bp.blogspot.com

"CITE" Gerald N. Hill and Kathleen T. Hill (1981-2005) online publication on Malice.

A web publication of 28th November 2012, defined debt burden as "The cost of interest payment on debt." www.economicshelp.org.

Oyedepo, Bishop David. *Breaking Financial Hardship*, 1995

Refinery 29 Publication "Divorce Rate in America 2017 Statistics, Marriage Today" Jan. 2017. 9.40pm. www.refinery29.com/2017/01/13744

Divorce Online Publications:
www.divorceonline.co.uk

Ramesh, Richard, *Scripture Sculpture*, Minnesota, Baker Books, 1995

Bruce, F.F. *The International Bible Commentary*, New Edition, 1986

Other Books Consulted During My Writing

Akpami, Clara A. *Handbook of Marriage* CTC Publication 2014

Wright, H. Norman. *Complete Guide To Trauma Counseling,* Minnesota, Bethany House, 2014

Renner, Rick. *Dressed To Kill: A Biblical Approach To Spiritual Warfare And Armor*, Tulsa, Teach All Nations, 2007

Gerrie, Greg A. *Fired Up For Life,* Victoria, Friesen Press, 2013

Thurman, Chris, *The Lies We Believe*, USA, Thomas Nelson, 1989

Martin, Walter. *The Kingdom Of The Cults*, Bethany House, 1996

Benson, Dan. *The Total Man*, Tyndale House, 1985

Ed Wheat, M.D. and Perkins, G. O. *Love Life For Every Married Couple,* Michigan, Zondervan, 1980

ABOUT THE AUTHOR

Dr. Godly Agala is first and foremost a child of God just like you are. He is by the Grace of God, a pastor, a preacher and a teacher of the word for over thirty years. He is down to earth and unambiguous in the way he presents the gospel.

God loves him so much, that there is nothing God cannot do for him. One time he was to be shot by a colonel but God made him invisible with his car in broad daylight.

He is a servant of God with a great passion for learning. He was a professional Landscape Architect who handled some sensitive landscape projects in the Federal Capital Territory Abuja, Nigeria.

After a second degree in Nigeria, he acquired his doctorate in Christian Philosophy in 2015 at Phoenix University of Theology, now Primus University, in the United States of America.

On his return to Nigeria, he became a licensed Mediator and Conciliator at the Nigeria Institute of Chartered Mediators And Conciliators.

He is presently Regional Overseer with the Christian Teaching Centre Family Church and the Director of Training for the Global Bible Training Institute, Abuja Campus.

He is a husband of one wife, Ndidi Paschaline. They live in the Federal Capital Territory Abuja Nigeria, with their six children: Prince, Princess, Prosper, Precious, Praise and Prisca.

Made in the USA
Lexington, KY
31 August 2018